Ira David Sankey, James McGranahan

Sacred Songs, No. 1

Ira David Sankey, James McGranahan

Sacred Songs, No. 1

ISBN/EAN: 9783337179960

Printed in Europe, USA, Canada, Australia, Japan

Cover: Foto ©Thomas Meinert / pixelio.de

More available books at **www.hansebooks.com**

CHRISTIAN ENDEAVOR EDITION

———— OF ————

SACRED SONGS
No. 1

BY

IRA D. SANKEY
JAMES MCGRANAHAN
AND GEO. C. STEBBINS

UNITED SOCIETY OF CHRISTIAN ENDEAVOR

BOSTON, MASS.
646 WASHINGTON STREET

CHICAGO HOUSE
155 LA SALLE STREET

THE BIGLOW & MAIN CO.

74 East 9th Street
New York

Lakeside Building
Chicago

COPYRIGHT, 1897, BY THE BIGLOW & MAIN CO.

PREFACE.

CHRISTIAN ENDEAVOR EDITION

OF

SACRED SONGS No. 1.

AT the request of the United Society of Christian Endeavor, Boston, Mass., this book has been prepared for the use of Endeavorers and Christian workers of every name, to the end that as far as possible the latest and best "Sacred Songs," together with the most popular "Gospel Hymns" and "C. E. Hymns," might be furnished in a single volume.

In this collection, "SACRED SONGS No. 1." has been supplemented by 32 pages of selected *Hymns, Scripture Readings, Topical Index, Motto, Pledge, Benediction, &c.*

We hope that those who use this collection will make an effort to learn the new songs therein, and not be content to sing only the old and more familiar pieces; by so doing, new interest will be created in the Service of Praise.

THE AUTHORS.

NOTICE.

Nearly all of the new pieces in this Collection, both words and music, are Copyright in the United States, Great Britain and Provinces, under the provisions of the International Copyright Law, and must not be reprinted or published for any purpose whatever, without the written permission of the owners thereof.

THE BIGLOW & MAIN CO., Publishers.

Christian Endeavor Edition
—— OF ——
Sacred Songs No. 1.

No. 1.   **Praise to the Holy One.**

"Unto thee will I sing * * * O thou Holy One of Israel."—Ps. 71:22.

LYMAN G. CUYLER.   RIAN A. DYKES.

1. Praise to the Ho-ly One, Je-sus our King; Songs of His
2. Sing how He bore the cross, Sing how He gave Free-ly, His
3. Sing of Him joy-ful-ly; Sing and pro-claim Hope to the

might-y love, Now let us sing; Lift we our joy-ful eyes,
pre-cious blood, Lost ones to save; Tell how He conquered death,
des-o-late, Rest thro' His name; Sing of His right-eous-ness,

Up to His throne; He hath cre-a-ted us, We are His own.
O wondrous love! Je-sus our Ad-vo-cate, Liv-eth a-bove.
Mer-cy, and love; Sing of the mansions bright, Waiting a-bove.

Copyright, 1896, by The Biglow & Main Co.

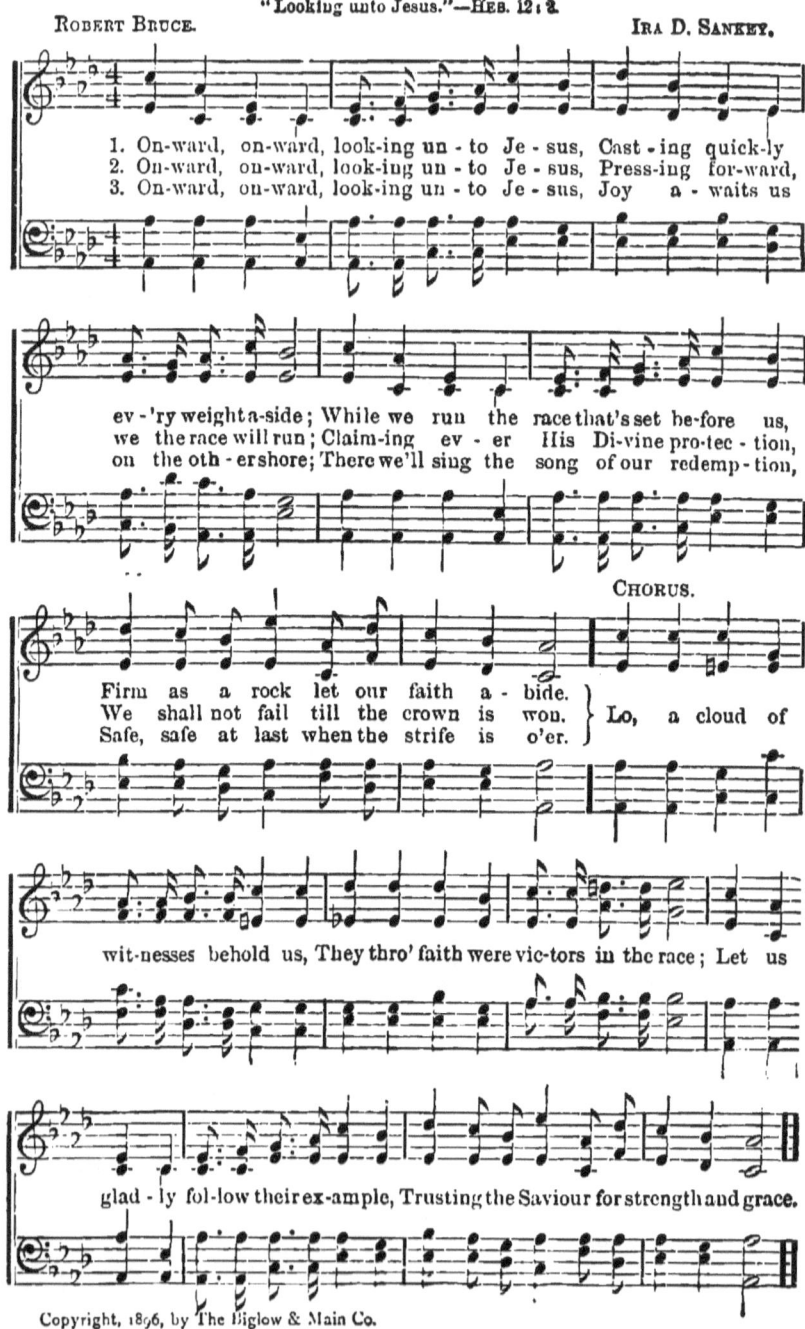

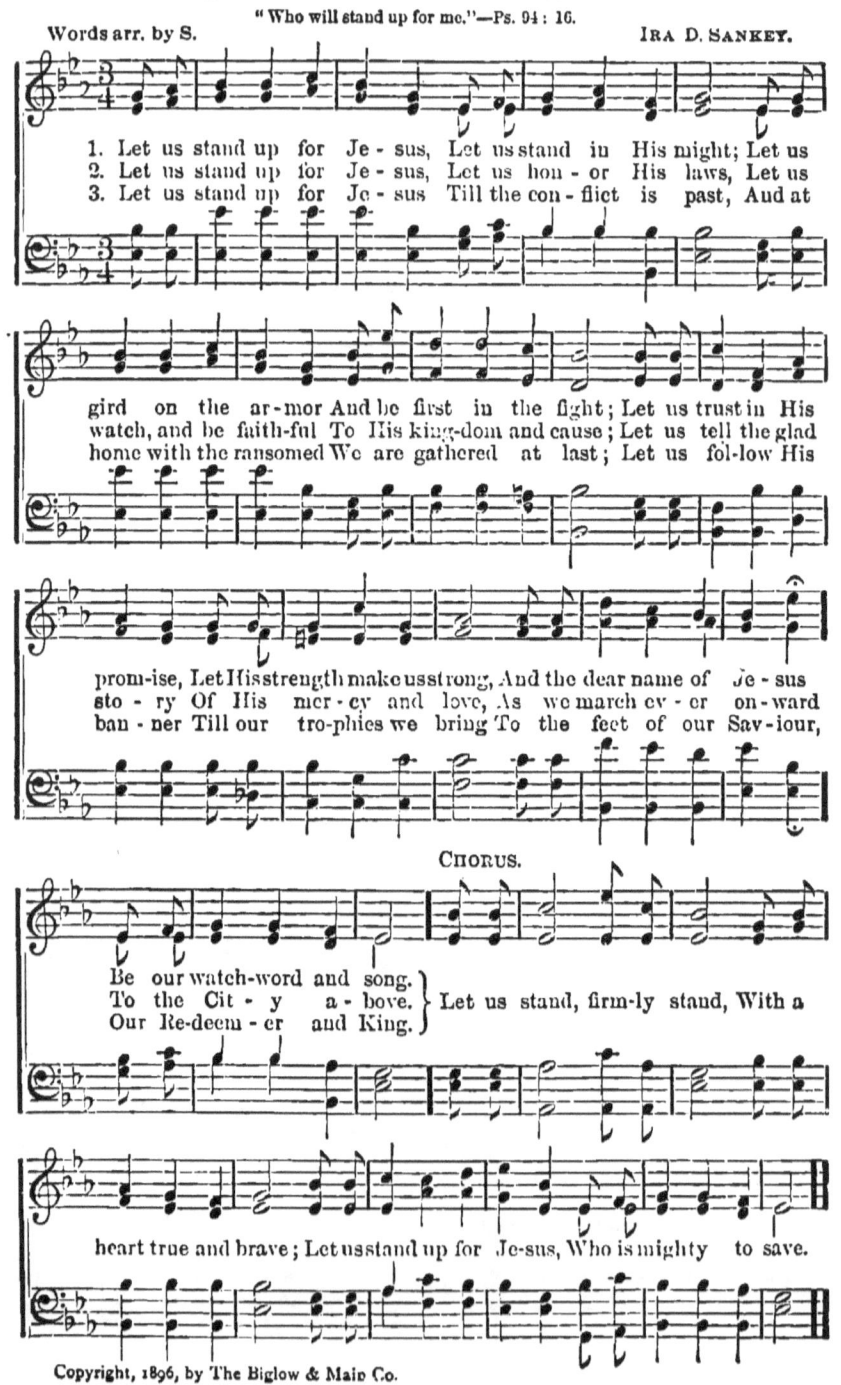

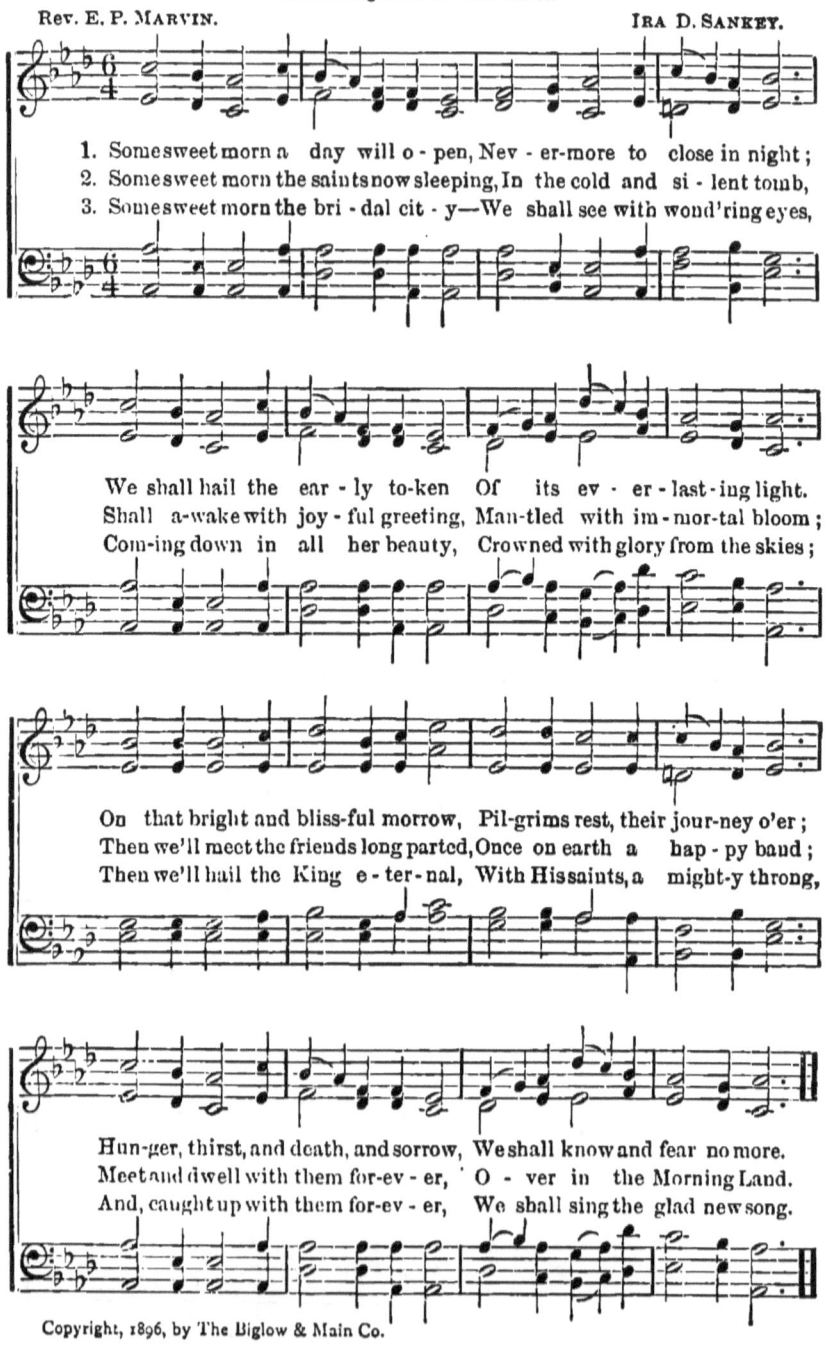

Come on the Wings.—Concluded.

dawn - ing, O come Thou Redeem-er and King.
come in the day that is dawning, O

No. 15. Comforted.

"Now he is comforted."—LUKE 16: 25.

M. FRASER.   M. A. SEA.

Moderato.

1. Aft - er a long and wea - ry strife, Aft - er a struggle 'twixt
2. Aft - er the night of dark - ness here, Aft - er the gloom, the
3. Aft - er the din and war of earth, Aft - er its wild, dis -
4. Aft - er the heart's deep ag - o - ny, Aft - er its yearning for

death and life, How sweet to feel the tem - pest cease, The
doubt, the fear, How sweet to hail heav'n's dawn-ing day, When
cord - ant mirth, How sweet to list the rapt - 'rous song That
sym - pa - thy, How pass - ing sweet will be the rest With -

an - gry bil - lows sink to peace, And per - fect calm be - gin.
ev - 'ry cloud is rolled a - way, And ev - 'ry eye sees clear.
ris - es from the white robed throng, Up - on the crys - tal sea.
in the arms, up - on the breast, Of Christ the Com - fort - er.

Copyright, 1896, by James McGranahan.

I will Trust,—Concluded.

strength and song; He al-so is be-come my sal-va-tion.

No. 21. Christ Alone is Saviour.

"For he shall save his people from their sins."—MATT. 1: 21.

Furnished by E. N.
M. A. SEA.

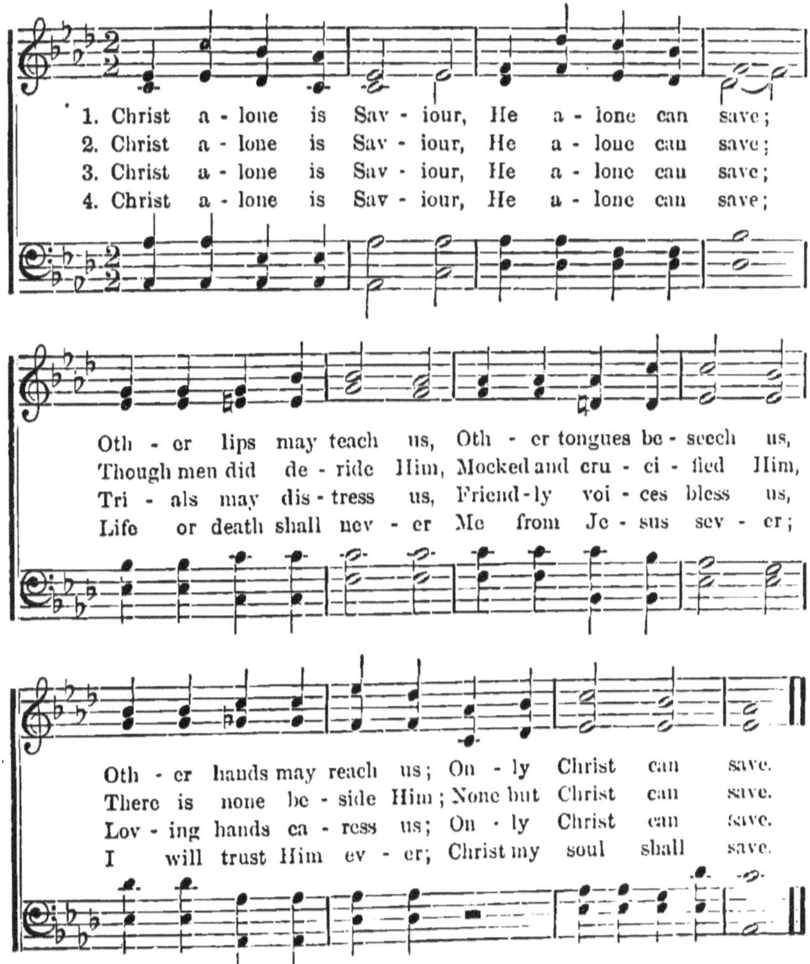

1. Christ a-lone is Sav-iour, He a-lone can save;
2. Christ a-lone is Sav-iour, He a-lone can save;
3. Christ a-lone is Sav-iour, He a-lone can save;
4. Christ a-lone is Sav-iour, He a-lone can save;

Oth-er lips may teach us, Oth-er tongues be-seech us,
Though men did de-ride Him, Mocked and cru-ci-fied Him,
Tri-als may dis-tress us, Friend-ly voi-ces bless us,
Life or death shall nev-er Me from Je-sus sev-er;

Oth-er hands may reach us; On-ly Christ can save.
There is none be-side Him; None but Christ can save.
Lov-ing hands ca-ress us; On-ly Christ can save.
I will trust Him ev-er; Christ my soul shall save.

Copyright, 1896, by James McGranahan.

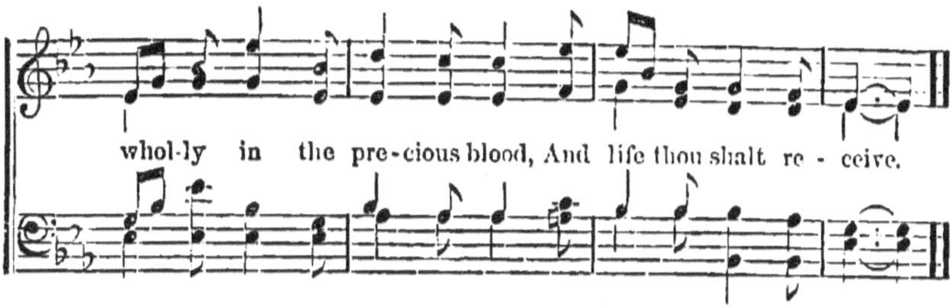

Say "Yes" to Jesus Now.—Concluded.

whol-ly in the pre-cious blood, And life thou shalt re - ceive.

No. 23. Spirit so Holy.

"Lead me in thy truth, and teach me."—Ps. 25:5.

D. W. WHITTLE.   GEO. C. STEBBINS.

1. Spir - it so ho - ly, Spir - it of love, Spir - it so
2. Spir - it of wis - dom, Spir - it of light, Spir - it of
3. Spir - it so hum - ble, Spir - it so meek, Spir - it so
4. Spir - it of pow - er, Spir - it of God, Spir - it of

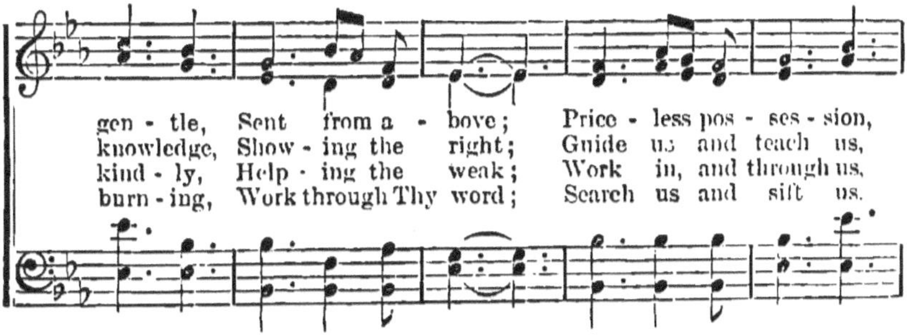

gen - tle, Sent from a - bove; Price - less pos - ses - sion,
knowledge, Show - ing the right; Guide us and teach us,
kind - ly, Help - ing the weak; Work in, and through us,
burn - ing, Work through Thy word; Search us and sift us.

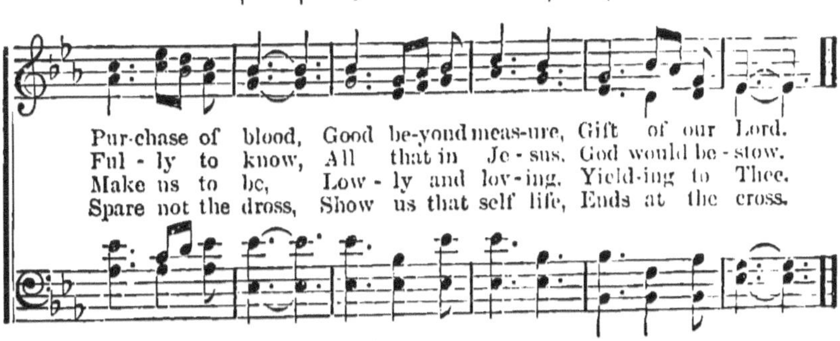

Pur-chase of blood, Good be-yond meas-ure, Gift of our Lord.
Ful - ly to know, All that in Je - sus, God would be - stow.
Make us to be, Low - ly and lov-ing. Yield-ing to Thee.
Spare not the dross, Show us that self life, Ends at the cross.

Copyright, 1896, by The Biglow & Main Co.

Morning Breaks,—Concluded.

No. 25. Counted Worthy.

"To suffer shame."—ACTS 5: 41.

M. FRASER. M. A. SEA.

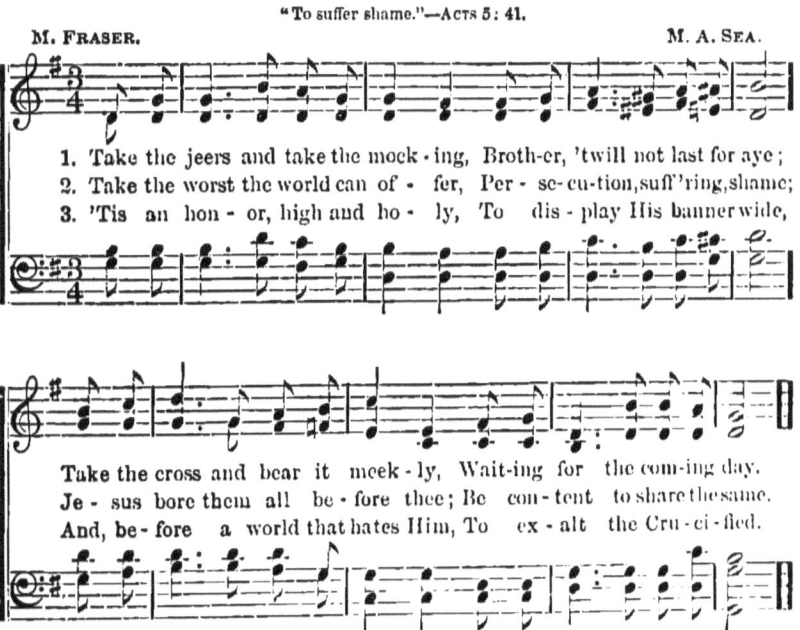

1. Take the jeers and take the mock-ing, Broth-er, 'twill not last for aye;
2. Take the worst the world can of-fer, Per-se-cu-tion, suff'ring, shame;
3. 'Tis an hon-or, high and ho-ly, To dis-play His banner wide,

Take the cross and bear it meek-ly, Wait-ing for the com-ing day.
Je-sus bore them all be-fore thee; Be con-tent to share the same.
And, be-fore a world that hates Him, To ex-alt the Cru-ci-fied.

Copyright, 1896, by James McGranahan.

No. 26. Blessed Saviour, Hear my Prayer.

"Give ear to my prayer."—Ps. 55: 1.

FRED. H. JACOBS.   GEO. C. STEBBINS.

1. Bless - ed Sav-iour, hear my pray'r, As I kneel be-fore Thee,
Plead - ing for Thy love and care; Spread Thy man-tle o'er me;
I have wan-dered from Thy fold, And my heart is wea - ry,
Trav-'ling thro' the storm and cold Of this des - ert drear - y.

2. All un - wor-thy though I be, Grant me, Lord, Thy fa - vor,
While I hum-bly bow the knee, Hear my pray'r, O Sav - iour;
For the sins that cause Thee pain, Give me deep con-tri - tion;
Speak Thy cleansing once a - gain, Pit - y my con - di - tion.

3. Thou dost hear the hum-blest cry Which in faith is spo - ken,
And the ra - diant, sun - lit sky Speaks Thy love un - bro - ken;
May I walk at Thy dear side, Ne'er from Thee to sev - er;
Let me, at Life's e - ven-tide, Dwell with Thee for - ev - er.

4. There I'll praise Thee for Thy *love* Which on earth has sought me,
Praise Thee with the hosts a - bove, For the *blood* that bought me;
For the match-less won-drous *grace* Which to me was giv - en,
And by which I won the race, Palm, and Crown, and Heav-en.

Copyright, 1896, by The Biglow & Main Co.

My Grace is Sufficient.—Concluded.

No. 29.

Make me Willing.

"Thy people shall be willing in the day of thy power."—Ps. 110: 3.

M. FRASER.　　　　　　　　　　　　　　　　　　　　　　　　M. A. SEA.

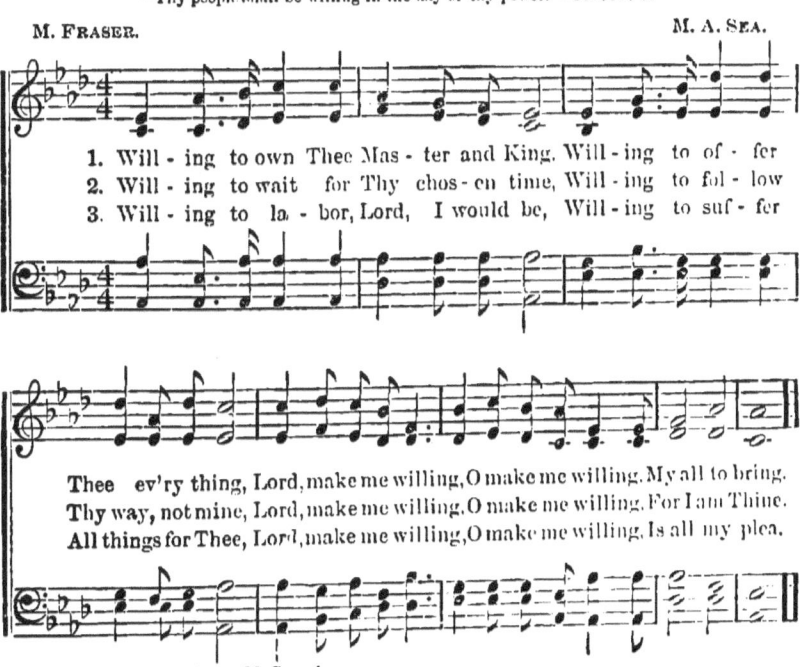

Copyright, 1896, by James McGranahan.

I Am the Light.—Concluded.

No. 33. **Be Near Me, O my Saviour.**

"I will never leave thee, nor forsake thee."—Heb. 13: 5.

EL. NATHAN. JAMES McGRANAHAN.

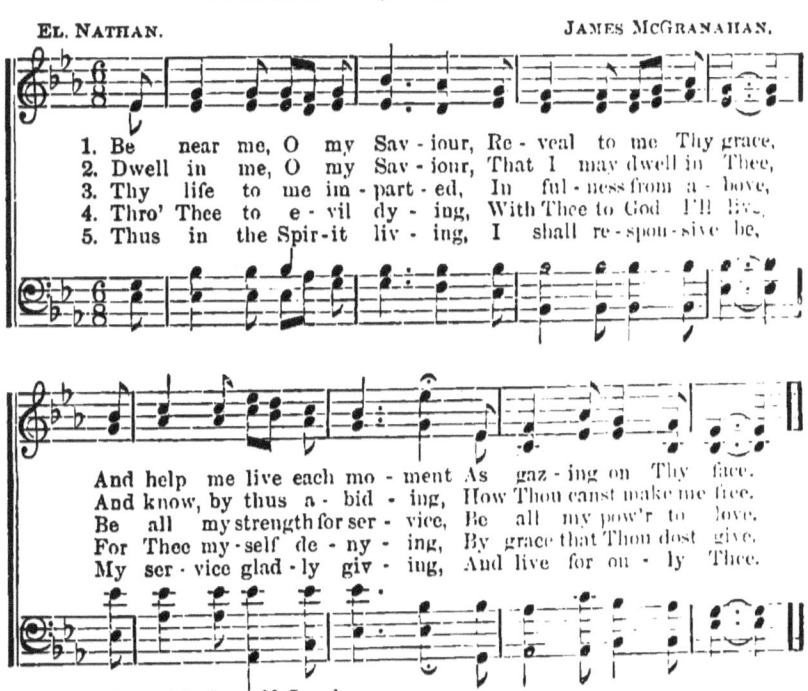

1. Be near me, O my Sav-iour, Re-veal to me Thy grace,
2. Dwell in me, O my Sav-iour, That I may dwell in Thee,
3. Thy life to me im-part-ed, In ful-ness from a-bove,
4. Thro' Thee to e-vil dy-ing, With Thee to God I'll live,
5. Thus in the Spir-it liv-ing, I shall re-spon-sive be,

And help me live each mo-ment As gaz-ing on Thy face.
And know, by thus a-bid-ing, How Thou canst make me free.
Be all my strength for ser-vice, Be all my pow'r to love.
For Thee my-self de-ny-ing, By grace that Thou dost give.
My ser-vice glad-ly giv-ing, And live for on-ly Thee.

Copyright, 1896, by James McGranahan.

No. 34. **Saved To-Night.**

"Wherefore he is able also to save to the uttermost." Heb. 7: 25.

Rev. E. A. FRIDENHAGEN.   IRA D. SANKEY.

1. Down in - to my lone - li - ness, sor - row and night, Il - lu - ming my soul with its ra - di-ance bright; There comes a sweet mes-sage of love and of light, That I may be saved to - night.
2. For years in the dark-ness of sin I have trod, Neg - lect - ing my Sav-iour, de - spis - ing His blood! A - way from my home, and a - way from my God, Yet I may be saved to - night.
3. I'm com - ing in weakness, my Sav - iour, to Thee, From sin and its bondage I long to be free; Re - ceive me O Mas - ter, Thine own would I be, And I shall be saved to - night.
4. The mes - sage of par - don at last I have heard, And take Thee as Sav - iour, Re - deem - er and Lord; I'll doubt Thee no lon - ger, but trust in Thy word, That I may be saved to - night.

REFRAIN.

That I may be saved to - night, That I may be saved to - night;
Yet I may be saved to - night, Yet I may be saved to - night;
And I shall be saved to - night, And I shall be saved to - night;
That I may be saved to - night, That I may be saved to - night;

Copyright, 1894, by The Biglow & Main Co.

No. 36. **Build Ye on the Rock.**

"The rock of salvation."—Ps. 89 : 26.

Mrs. C. E. Breck.   J. H. Burke.

1. Build ye on the Rock foun-da-tion, And thy house shall sure-ly stand
2. Build ye on the Rock foun-da-tion, Build with purpose true and brave;
3. Build ye on the Rock foun-da-tion, Cor-ner stone of wondrous love;

When the storm brings des-o-la-tion To the house built on the sand.
Build a glo-rious hab-it-a-tion, Strong to shel-ter, strong to save.
In thy day of ex-alt-a-tion, Thou shalt dwell with Christ above.

CHORUS.

Build ye on . . . the Rock founda-tion, On the Rock . . that standeth sure—
on the Rock foun - da-tion, Rock that stand-eth sure—

On the Rock of God's sal - va - tion, That for-ev - er shall en-dure.
That for-ev-er shall en - dure.

Copyright, 1896, by The Biglow & Main Co.

No. 37. **My Hiding Place.**

"Thou art my hiding place."—Ps. 32: 7.

R. HUTCHINSON. IRA D. SANKEY.

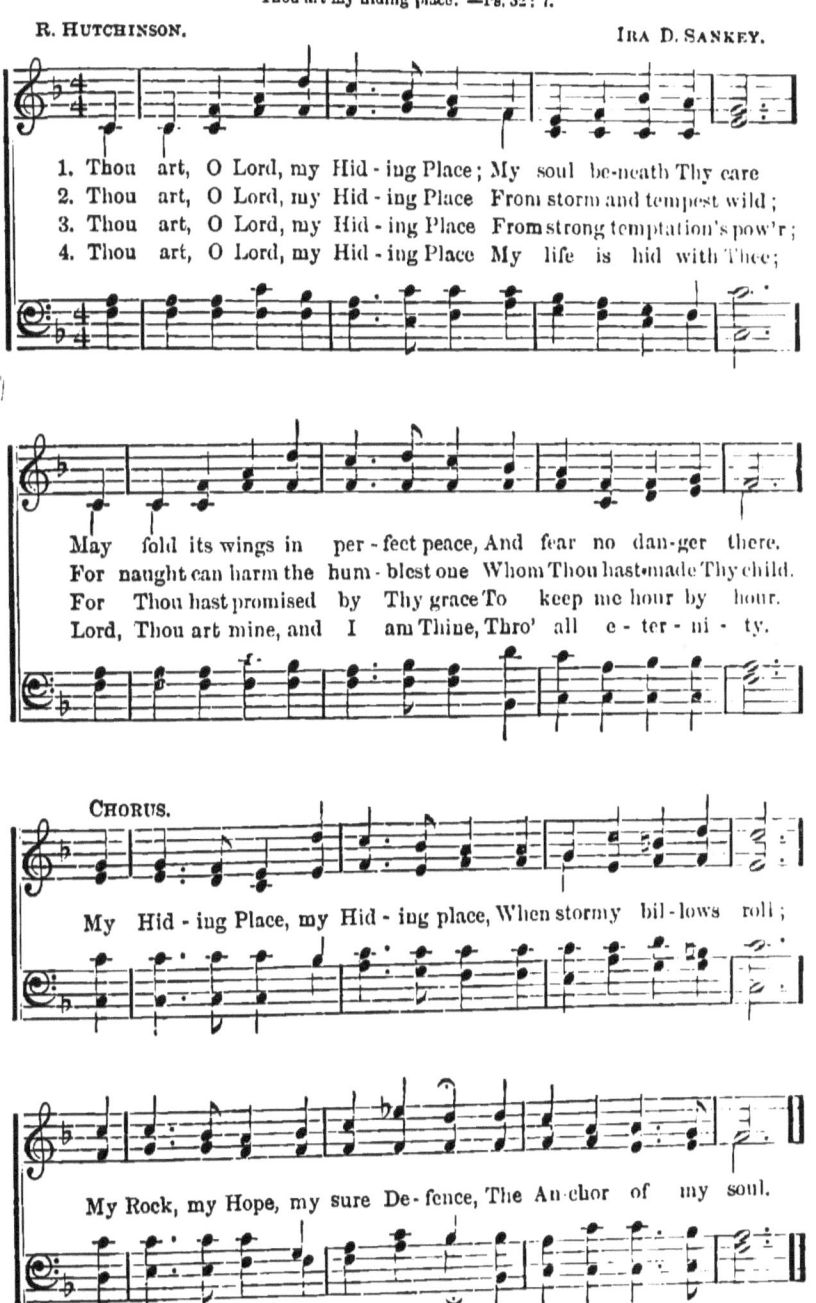

1. Thou art, O Lord, my Hid-ing Place; My soul be-neath Thy care
2. Thou art, O Lord, my Hid-ing Place From storm and tempest wild;
3. Thou art, O Lord, my Hid-ing Place From strong temptation's pow'r;
4. Thou art, O Lord, my Hid-ing Place My life is hid with Thee;

May fold its wings in per-fect peace, And fear no dan-ger there.
For naught can harm the hum-blest one Whom Thou hast made Thy child.
For Thou hast promised by Thy grace To keep me hour by hour.
Lord, Thou art mine, and I am Thine, Thro' all e-ter-ni-ty.

CHORUS.

My Hid-ing Place, my Hid-ing place, When stormy bil-lows roll;

My Rock, my Hope, my sure De-fence, The An-chor of my soul.

Copyright, 1896, by The Biglow & Main Co.

When Jesus Comes Again.—Concluded.

CHORUS.

When Je - sus comes a - gain, When Je - sus comes a - gain,
O day of joy and glad-ness, When Je - sus comes a - gain.

No. 39.   Christ has Risen.

"My Lord and my God."—JOHN 20 : 28.

M. FRASER.   M. A SEA.
With spirit.

1. Christ has ris - en from the dead, He who suf-fered in our stead;
2. They who sang when He was born, Sing a - gain this Eas - ter morn,
3. He has burst the captive's chain; Now they glo - ry in His name
4. See, the tomb has o - pened wide; See, the Lord, who bled and died,
5. On that grand tri - umph-ant day, When things old shall pass a - way,
6. Christ the first fruits now we see, Of a har - vest yet to be,

Rise we with our ris - en Head; Al - le - lu - iah! al - le - lu - iah!
Songs that glad-den hearts for - lorn; Al - le - lu - iah! al - le - lu - iah!
Who for them did suf - fer shame; Al - le - lu - iah! al - le - lu - iah!
Now has ris - en glo - ri - fied; Al - le - lu - iah! al - le - lu - iah!
We shall lift our voice and say, Al - le - lu - iah! al - le - lu - iah!
When we're gathered, Lord, to Thee. Al - le - lu - iah! al - le - lu - iah!

Copyright, 1896, by James McGranahan.

Comfort Ye One Another.—Concluded.

Com-fort ye one an-oth - er with . . . these words . . .
one an-oth-er these words.

No. 43. Go Tell it to Jesus.

"And his disciples * * * * went and told Jesus."—MATT. 14: 12.

M. A. BACHELOR, alt.   HARRY S. LOWER.

1. Go bur-y thy sor-row, The world has its share: Go bur-y it
2. Go tell it to Je-sus, He know-eth thy grief; Go tell it to
3. Hearts growing a-wea-ry With heav-i-er woe Now droop 'mid the

deep - ly, Go hide it with care; Go think of it calm-ly, When
Je - sus, He'll send thee re - lief, Go gath-er the sun-shine He
dark-ness—Go com-fort them, go; Go bur-y thy sor-row, Let

cur-tain'd by night, Go tell it to Je-sus, And all will be right.
sheds on the way; He'll lighten thy bur-den, Go, wea-ry one, pray.
oth - ers be blest; Go give them the sunshine—Tell Je-sus the rest.

Copyright, 1894, by The Biglow & Main Co.

No. 44. Sunshine in the Soul.

"I will joy in the God of my salvation."—Hab. 3:18.

E. E. Hewitt. Jno. R. Sweney.

1. There's sunshine in my soul to-day, More glo-ri-ous and bright
2. There's mu-sic in my soul to-day, A car-ol to my King,
3. There's springtime in my soul to-day, For when the Lord is near,
4. There's gladness in my soul to-day, And hope, and praise, and love,

Than glows in an-y earth-ly sky, For Je-sus is the Light.
And Je-sus, list-en-ing, can hear The songs I can-not sing.
The dove of peace sings in my heart, The flow'rs of grace ap-pear.
For blessings which He gives me now, For joys laid up a-bove.

Refrain.

Oh, there's sun - - shine, Bless-ed sun - - shine,
sun-shine in my soul, sun-shine in my soul,

While the peace-ful, hap-py moments roll; When
hap-py mo-ments roll,

Je-sus shows His smil-ing face, There is sunshine in my soul.

Copyright, 1887, by Jno. R. Sweney. Used by per.

Pleasures Forevermore.—Concluded.

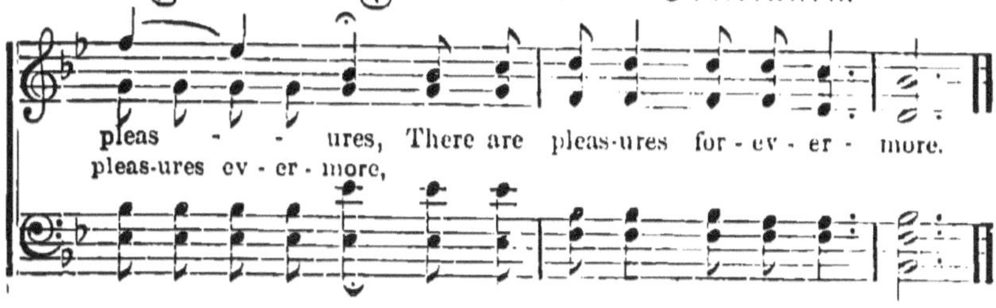

pleas - - ures, There are pleas-ures for - ev - er - more.
pleas-ures ev - er - more,

No. 47. Keep Thou My Way.

"The LORD is thy keeper."—Ps. 121 : 5.

F. J. CROSBY.　　　　　　　　　　　　　　　　THEO. E. PERKINS.

1. Keep Thou my way, O Lord, Be Thou ev - er nigh; Strong is Thy
2. Keep Thou my heart, O Lord, Ev - er close to Thee; Safe in Thine
3. Keep Thou my all, O Lord, Hide my life in Thine; O let Thy

might - y arm, Weak and frail am I; Thou, my un-chang-ing Friend,
arms of love, Shall my ref - uge be; Then, o'er a tran - quil tide,
sa - cred light O'er my pathway shine; Kept by Thy ten - der care,

On Thee my hopes depend; Till life's brief day shall end, Be Thou ever nigh.
My bark shall safely glide; I shall be sat - is - fied, Ever close to Thee.
Gladly the cross I'll bear; Hear Thou and grant my pray'r, Hide my life in Thine.

Copyright, 1894, by The Biglow & Main Co,

No. 50. Abide with me Ever.

"Abide with us, for it is toward evening."—LUKE 24:29.

JOHN H. YATES.   GEO. C. STEBBINS.

1. With-out Thee, my Sav-iour, I noth-ing can do; I strive, but I fail to be faith-ful and true; My strength is but weak-ness, and faint is my heart, Un-less Thou art nigh me Thy grace to im-part.
2. With-out Thee, my Sav-iour, I strug-gle in vain; I sink 'neath the wave with no arm to sus-tain; But when Thou art with me to strengthen my soul, I cling to the Rock though the waves o'er me roll.
3. With-out Thee, my Sav-iour, I can-not pre-vail When foes of my soul with their weap-ons as-sail; But when Thou art with me to gird me with might, I march to the bat-tle, and win in the fight.

CHORUS.

A-bide...... with me ev - - er, O Sav - iour, a-bide,.... My Ref - - uge in
A-bide, O a-bide, ev-er a-bide,. Saviour, O Sav-iour with me a-bide, My Ref-uge in dan-ger, my

Copyright, 1896, by The Biglow & Main Co.

Abide with me Ever.—Concluded.

dan - - ger, in dark - - ness, my Guide. . . .
Ref - uge in dan - ger, in dark-ness my Guide, in darkness my Guide.

No. 51. How Long?

"At evening time it shall be light."—ZECH. 14: 7.

SARAH DOUDNEY, arr. IRA D. SANKEY.

1. The wea-ry hours like shadows come and go, As still I strive, by
2. But are there ma-ny wea-ry miles to tread Be-fore the prom-ised
3. Some lit-tle joy I have in do-ing still The hum-ble work He
4. And thus the days are slow-ly pass-ing here, With distant gleams of
5. Ah, yes, when that great light which men call Death Strikes thro' the gloom and

earn-est faith and pray'r: To do each day the du-ties that I know,
home ap-pears in sight? And are there sad and bit-ter tears to shed
bids me do for Him; A ten-der glad-ness when 'tis mine to fill
hope and glo-ry blest; But is the hal-lowed mo-ment drawing near
stills at last the strife, Then comes a hush, a sigh, a fleet-ing breath,

rit.

And bear the Cross my Sav-iour bids me bear.
Ere we shall meet in realms of end - less light?
A - gain some emp - ty chal - ice to the brim.
When we shall meet a - gain in end - less rest?
And we shall meet a - gain in end - less life.

Copyright, 1896, by The Biglow & Main Co.

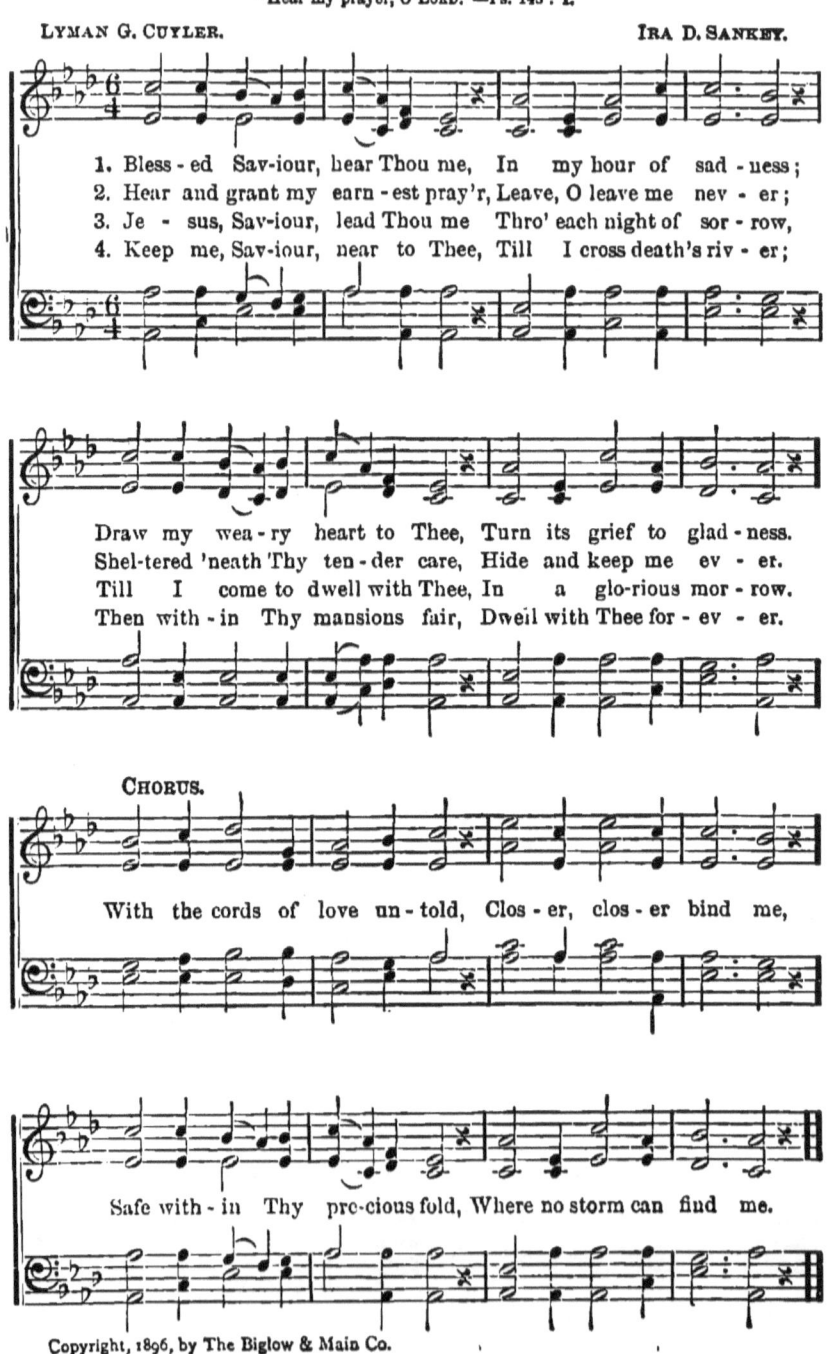

Where the Saviour Leads.—Concluded.

fol - low, Where the lov-ing Saviour leads me, I will gladly go.
glad-ly fol-low,

No. 59. **O How Happy Are They.**

"Happy is that people whose God is the Lord."—Ps. 144:15.

CHARLES WESLEY. Arr. H. P. M.

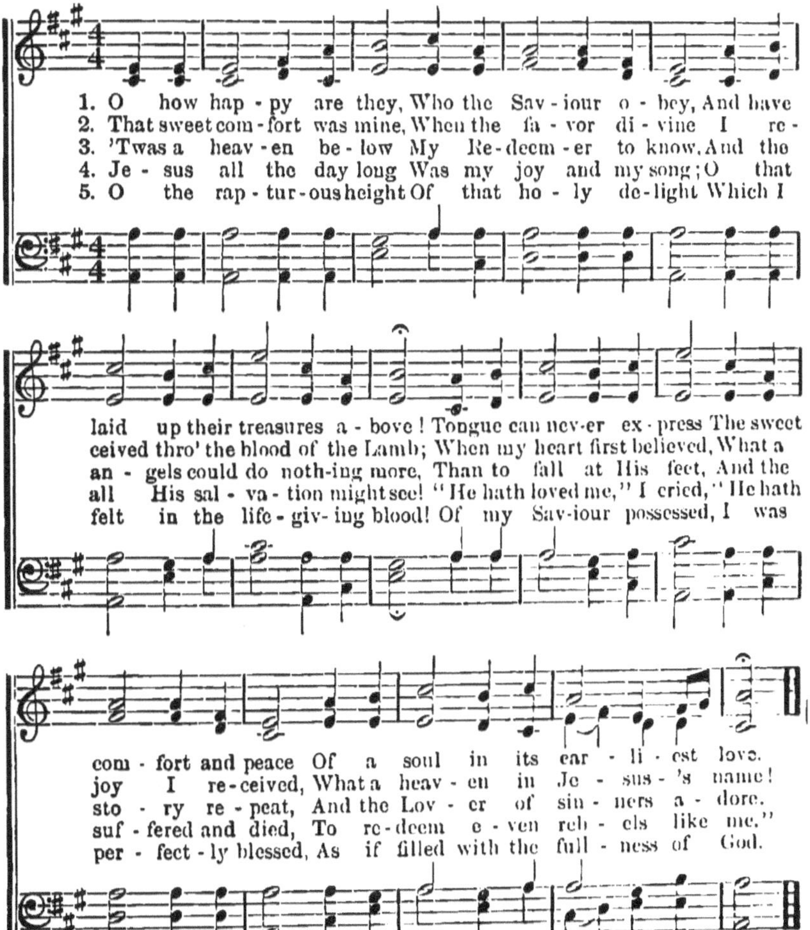

1. O how hap - py are they, Who the Sav - iour o - bey, And have
2. That sweet com - fort was mine, When the fa - vor di - vine I re -
3. 'Twas a heav - en be - low My Re - deem - er to know, And the
4. Je - sus all the day long Was my joy and my song ; O that
5. O the rap - tur - ous height Of that ho - ly de - light Which I

laid up their treasures a - bove ! Tongue can nev - er ex - press The sweet
ceived thro' the blood of the Lamb; When my heart first believed, What a
an - gels could do noth-ing more, Than to fall at His feet, And the
all His sal - va - tion might see! "He hath loved me," I cried, "He hath
felt in the life - giv - ing blood! Of my Sav - iour possessed, I was

com - fort and peace Of a soul in its ear - li - est love.
joy I re - ceived, What a heav - en in Je - sus - 's name!
sto - ry re - peat, And the Lov - er of sin - ners a - dore.
suf - fered and died, To re - deem e - ven reb - els like me."
per - fect - ly blessed, As if filled with the full - ness of God.

No. 62. Create in Me a Clean Heart.

"O God; and renew a right spirit within me."—Ps. 51: 10.

MARY B. WINGATE.   JAMES MCGRANAHAN.

1. My soul is sad and sin-ful; O Fa-ther, hear me pray;
2. O cast my sins be-hind Thee, Re-mem-ber them no more;
3. For-give, O lov-ing Sav-iour, My un-be-lief and sin;
4. O give the oil of glad-ness, Ac-cept the gift I bring;

Take from my heart this bur-den, And bear it far a-way.
Look on Thine own A-noint-ed, The Christ whom I a-dore.
My soul is wait-ing, long-ing, Thy courts to en-ter in.
Then I will chant Thy prais-es, Thy glo-ry will I sing.

CHORUS.

Cre-ate..... in me..... a clean heart, O God;
Cre-ate in me, in me

(Do not hurry.)

re-new a right spir-it with-in me. Wash me thor-ough-ly from mine in-i-qui-ty; cleanse me from my sin.

Copyright, 1896, by James McGranahan.

No. 66. Immanuel, Prince of Peace.

"Him hath God exalted to be a Prince and a Saviour."—Acts 5: 31.

ANDREW SHERWOOD.   D. B. TOWNER.

1. Oh, sing that song to me a-gain, Whose charm doth nev-er cease,
Of Him who died for sin-ful men: Im-man-uel, Prince of Peace;
The peer-less One of all the throng Who've walked our earthly sod;
The sweet-est name that lives in song: Christ Je-sus, Son of God.

2. When I, a lisp-ing in-fant, lay Up - on my mother's knee,
She told me in the twilight gray, How Je-sus died for me;
She sang a song of heav'n and God I nev - er can for - get;
And tho' she sleeps be-neath the sod, Her song is liv - ing yet.

3. Oh, song of songs, that grows sublime As on - ward roll the years;
Oh, sto - ry wov-en in - to rhyme, That melts the heart to tears;
I love, I love to hear that song, It fills my soul with joy;
To Him all songs of praise be-long Which mor-tal tongues em-ploy.

CHORUS.

Oh, sing that song to me a - gain, Whose charm doth nev-er cease,

Copyright, 1896, by D. B. Towner. Used by per.

Immanuel, Prince of Peace.—Concluded.

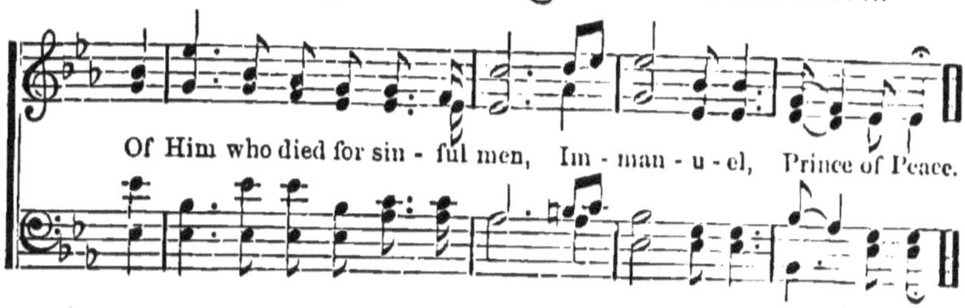

Of Him who died for sin-ful men, Im-man-u-el, Prince of Peace.

No. 67. Lord, I'm Coming Home.

"Come unto me all ye that labor."—MATT. 11:28.

W. J. K.
WM. J. KIRKPATRICK.

1. I've wandered far a-way from God, Now I'm coming home;
2. I've wast-ed ma-ny pre-cious years, Now I'm coming home;
3. I'm tired of sin and stray-ing, Lord, Now I'm coming home;
4. My soul is sick, my heart is sore, Now I'm coming home;

The paths of sin too long I've trod, Lord, I'm coming home.
I now re-pent with bit-ter tears, Lord, I'm coming home.
I'll trust Thy love, be-lieve Thy word, Lord, I'm coming home.
My strength re-new, my hope re-store, Lord, I'm coming home.

D.S.—*O-pen wide Thine arms of love, Lord, I'm coming home.*

CHORUS.

Com-ing home, com-ing home, Nev-er-more to roam;

5 My only hope, my only plea,
  Now I'm coming home,
That Jesus died, and died for me,
  Lord, I'm coming home.

6 I need His cleansing blood I know,
  Now I'm coming home;
Oh, wash me whiter than the snow,
  Lord, I'm coming home.

Copyright, 1892, by Wm. J. Kirkpatrick. Used by per.

Life is Mine.—Concluded.

made me free, Since He made me free....
Him be-long, And to Him be-long....
ev-er beam, Doth for-ev-er beam....
vic-t'ry won, The vic-t'ry won....

And my heart is glad since He made me free.
I am His a-lone, and to Him be-long.
On my path His light doth for-ev-er beam.
When the bat-tle's o'er, and the vic-t'ry won.

CHORUS.

Life is mine, faith is mine, strength is mine, Love is
Life is mine, faith is mine,

mine thro' the blood of the Lamb; Peace is mine, joy is
Peace is mine,

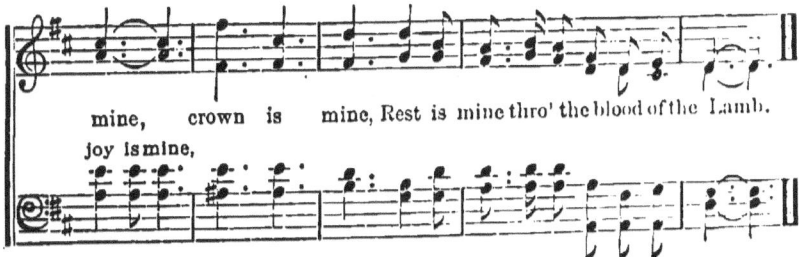

mine, crown is mine, Rest is mine thro' the blood of the Lamb.
joy is mine,

Eye Hath Not Seen.—Concluded.

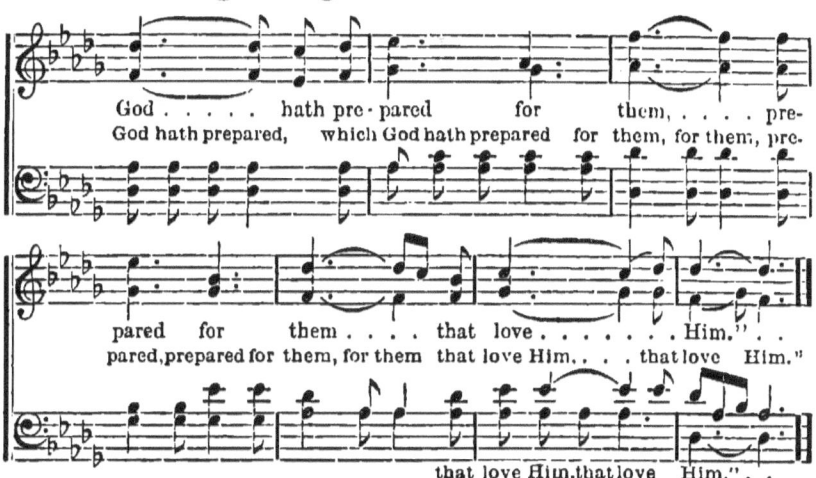

God .... hath pre-pared   for   them, ... pre-
God hath prepared, which God hath prepared for them, for them, pre-

pared   for   them .... that love ...... Him."..
pared, prepared for them, for them that love Him.... that love Him."

that love Him, that love Him."..

No. 70. Near to Thee.

"He will draw nigh to you."—JAMES 4: 8.

JULIA STERLING.   IRA D. SANKEY.

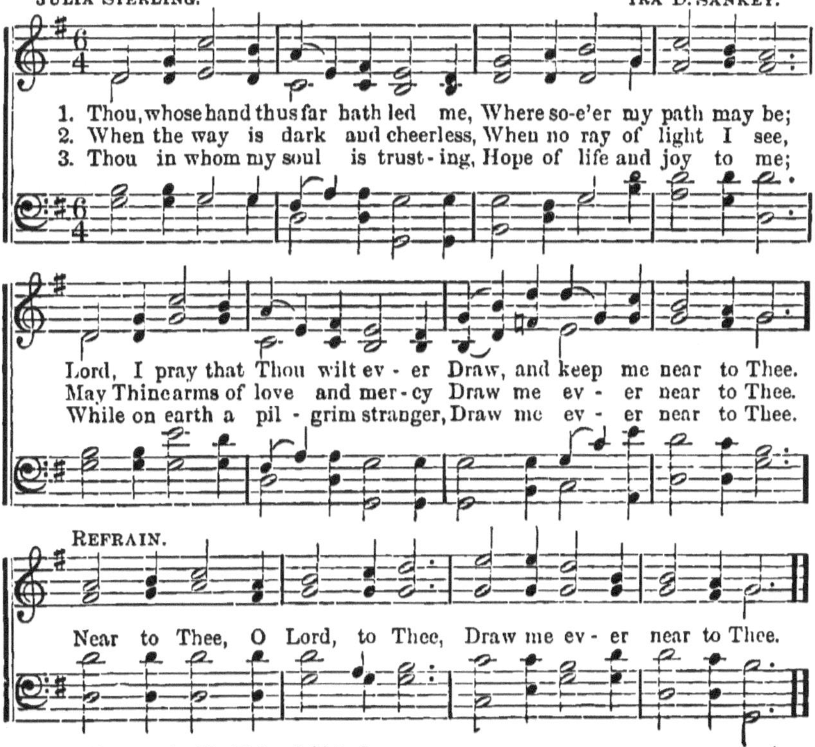

1. Thou, whose hand thus far hath led me, Where so-e'er my path may be;
2. When the way is dark and cheerless, When no ray of light I see,
3. Thou in whom my soul is trust-ing, Hope of life and joy to me;

Lord, I pray that Thou wilt ev - er Draw, and keep me near to Thee.
May Thine arms of love and mer-cy Draw me ev - er near to Thee.
While on earth a pil - grim stranger, Draw me ev - er near to Thee.

REFRAIN.

Near to Thee, O Lord, to Thee, Draw me ev - er near to Thee.

Copyright, 1896, by The Biglow & Main Co.

When the King.—Concluded.

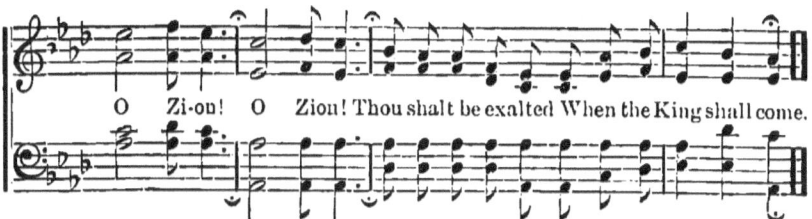

O Zi-on! O Zion! Thou shalt be exalted When the King shall come.

No. 76. Give your Heart to Jesus.

"My son, give me thine heart."—Prov. 23 : 26.

CHARLES BRUCE.   GEO. C. STEBBINS.

1. Would you be for - ev - er blest? Give your heart to Je - sus;
2. Would you dwell in heav'n a - bove? Give your heart to Je - sus;
3. Now His pard'ning grace re - ceive, Give your heart to Je - sus;

Would you find the balm of rest? Give your heart to Je - sus.
Would you meet with those you love? Give your heart to Je - sus.
On His pre-cious name be-lieve, Give your heart to Je - sus.

CHORUS.

Do not lin - ger, do not wait; Yon - der stands the o - pen gate;

En - ter ere it be too late; Give your heart to Je - sus.

Copyright, 1896, by The Biglow & Main Co.

He Feedeth His Flock.—Concluded.

No. 80. After the Darkest Hour.

"Joy cometh in the morning."—Ps. 30: 5.

Mrs. M. R. Tilden.   Ira D. Sankey.

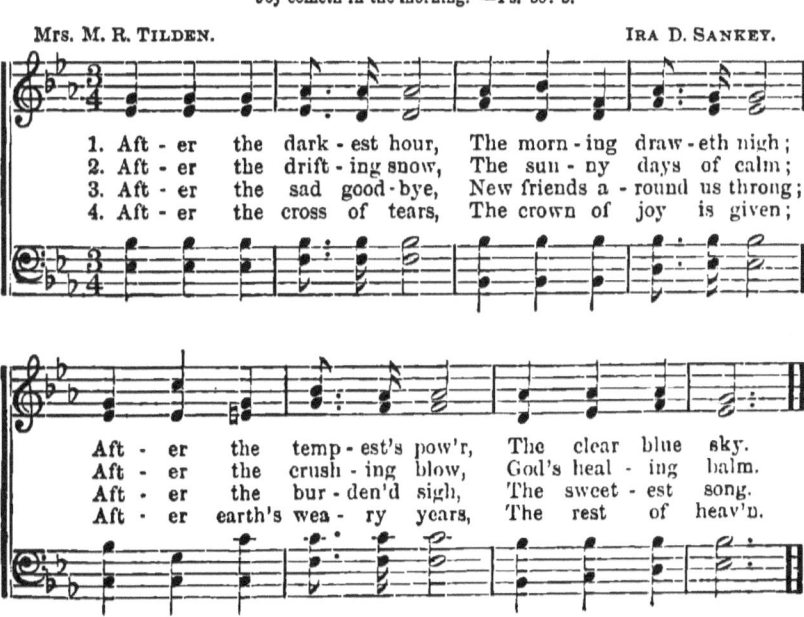

1. After the darkest hour, The morning draweth nigh;
2. After the drifting snow, The sunny days of calm;
3. After the sad good-bye, New friends around us throng;
4. After the cross of tears, The crown of joy is given;

After the tempest's pow'r, The clear blue sky.
After the crushing blow, God's healing balm.
After the burden'd sigh, The sweetest song.
After earth's weary years, The rest of heav'n.

Copyright, 1896, by The Biglow & Main Co.

O Sing of my Redeemer.—Concluded.

Up - on .... the cross He suf - fered,
the cross He suf - fered, on the cross He suf - fered,

From sin .... to set me free (to set me free).
to set me free,

No. 84. I Come, O Blessed Lord.

"Him that cometh to me I will in no wise cast out."—JOHN 6: 37.

ELLEN K. BRADFORD. IRA D. SANKEY.

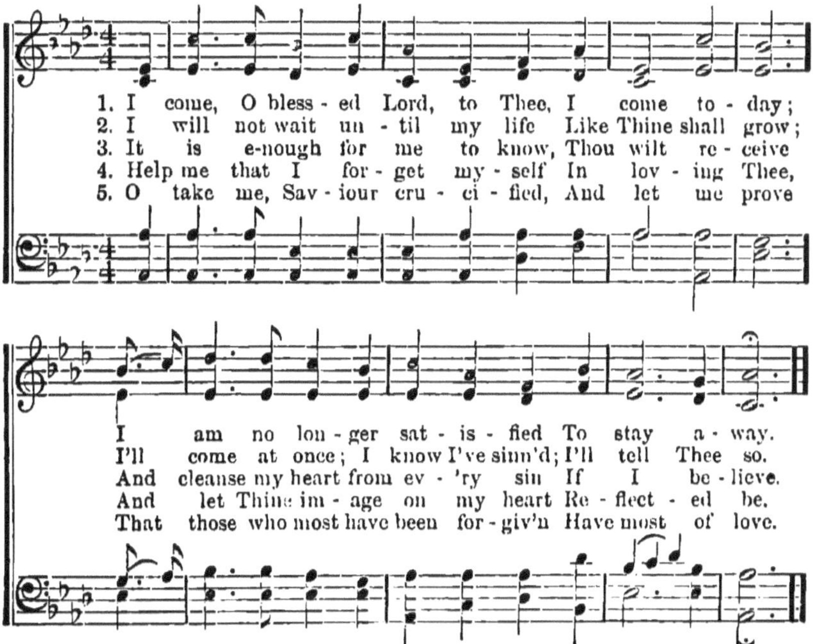

1. I come, O bless - ed Lord, to Thee, I come to - day;
2. I will not wait un - til my life Like Thine shall grow;
3. It is e-nough for me to know, Thou wilt re - ceive
4. Help me that I for - get my - self In lov - ing Thee,
5. O take me, Sav - iour cru - ci - fied, And let me prove

I am no lon - ger sat - is - fied To stay a - way.
I'll come at once; I know I've sinn'd; I'll tell Thee so.
And cleanse my heart from ev - 'ry sin If I be - lieve.
And let Thine im - age on my heart Re - flect - ed be.
That those who most have been for - giv'n Have most of love.

Copyright, 1896, by The Biglow & Main Co.

Are You a Reaper?—Concluded.

fruit.... un-to life ev-er-more? Lift up your eyes for the
fruit, golden fruit un-to life ev-er-more?
har-vest is read-y; Hast-en, oh, hast-en to gath-er your store.

No. 86.   ## God's Bounty.

"God is able to make all grace abound toward you."—2 Cor. 9:8.

ARATUS M. DEUEL.   M. A. SEA.

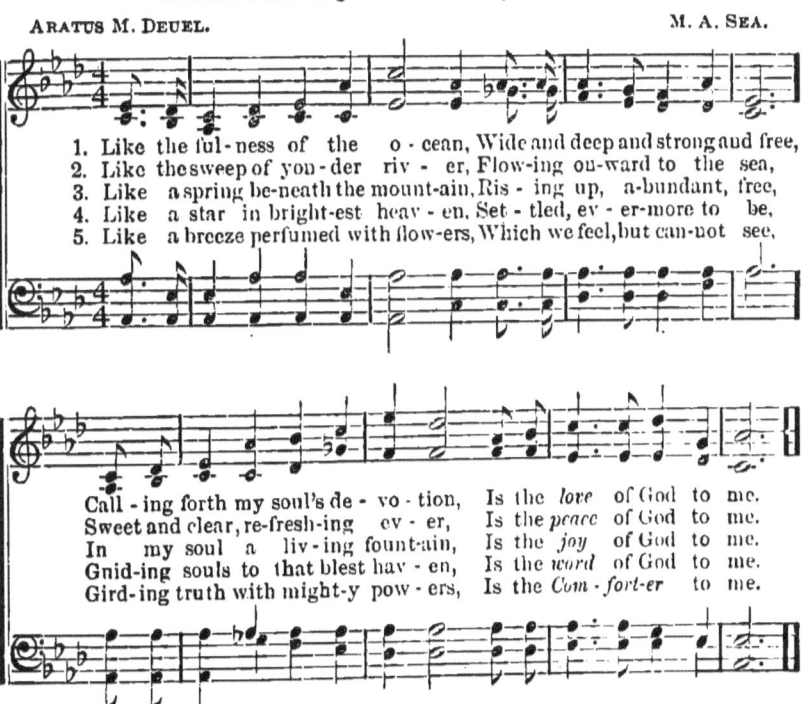

1. Like the ful-ness of the o-cean, Wide and deep and strong and free,
2. Like the sweep of yon-der riv-er, Flow-ing on-ward to the sea,
3. Like a spring be-neath the mount-ain, Ris-ing up, a-bundant, free,
4. Like a star in bright-est heav-en, Set-tled, ev-er-more to be,
5. Like a breeze perfumed with flow-ers, Which we feel, but can-not see,

Call-ing forth my soul's de-vo-tion,   Is the *love* of God to me.
Sweet and clear, re-fresh-ing ev-er,   Is the *peace* of God to me.
In my soul a liv-ing fount-ain,   Is the *joy* of God to me.
Gnid-ing souls to that blest hav-en,   Is the *word* of God to me.
Gird-ing truth with might-y pow-ers,   Is the *Com-fort-er* to me.

Copyright, 1896, by James McGranahan.

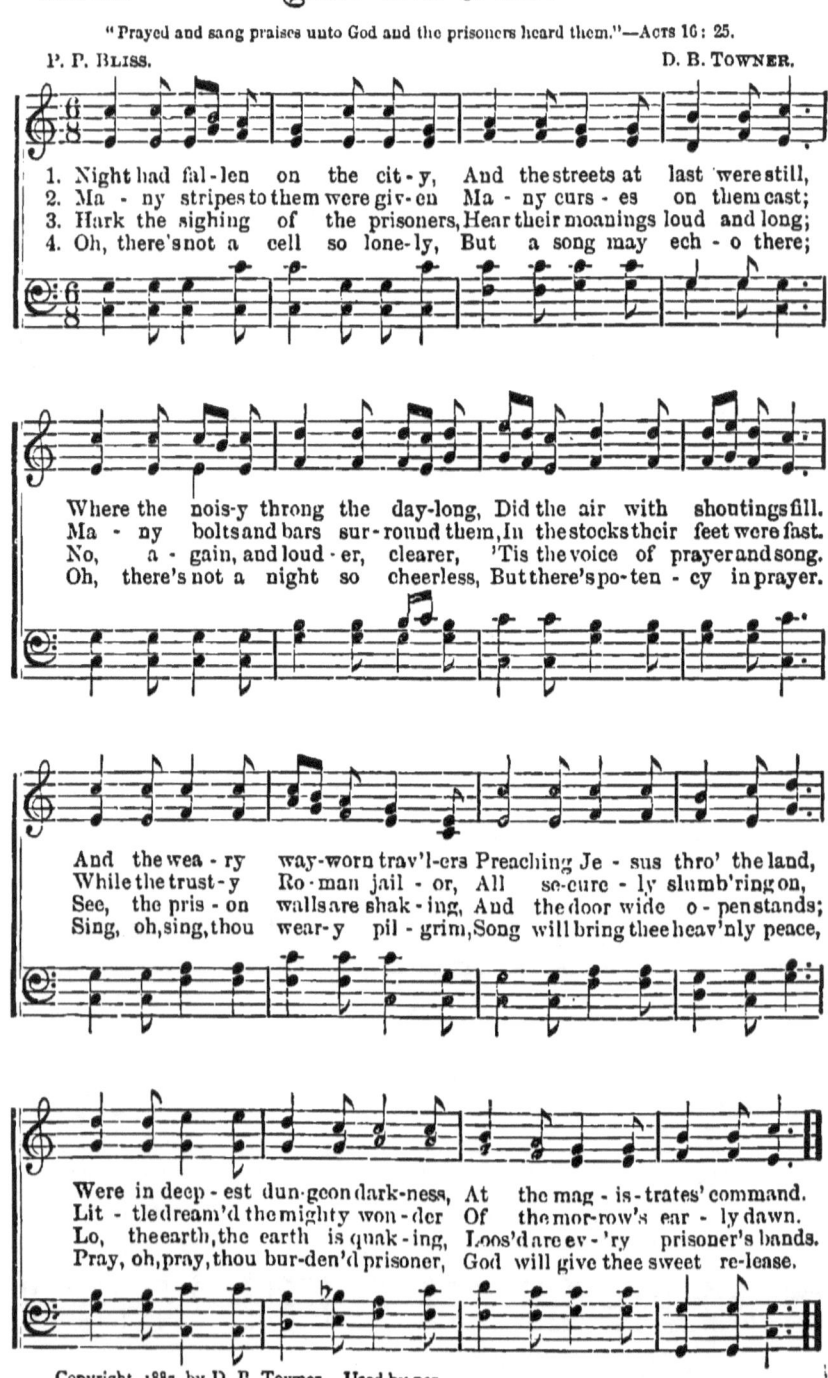

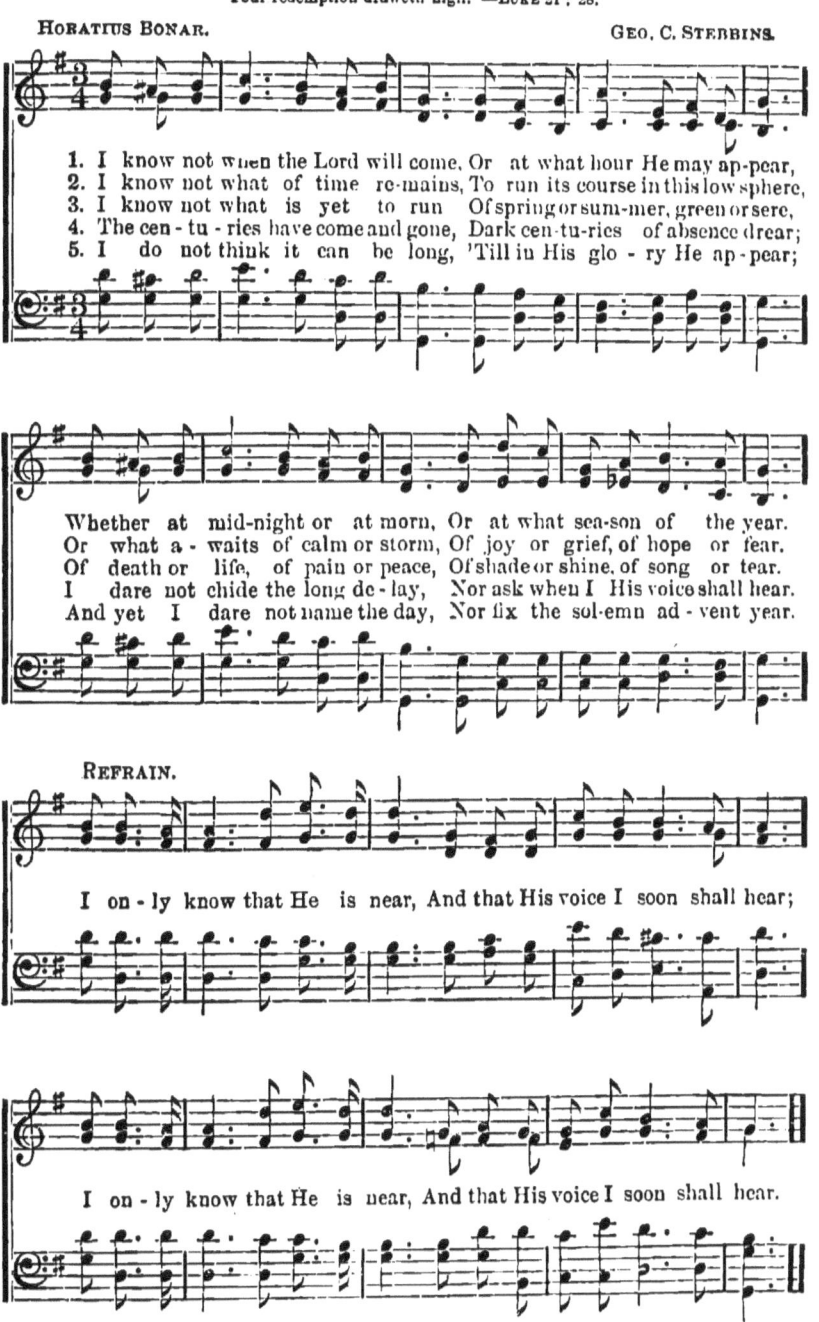

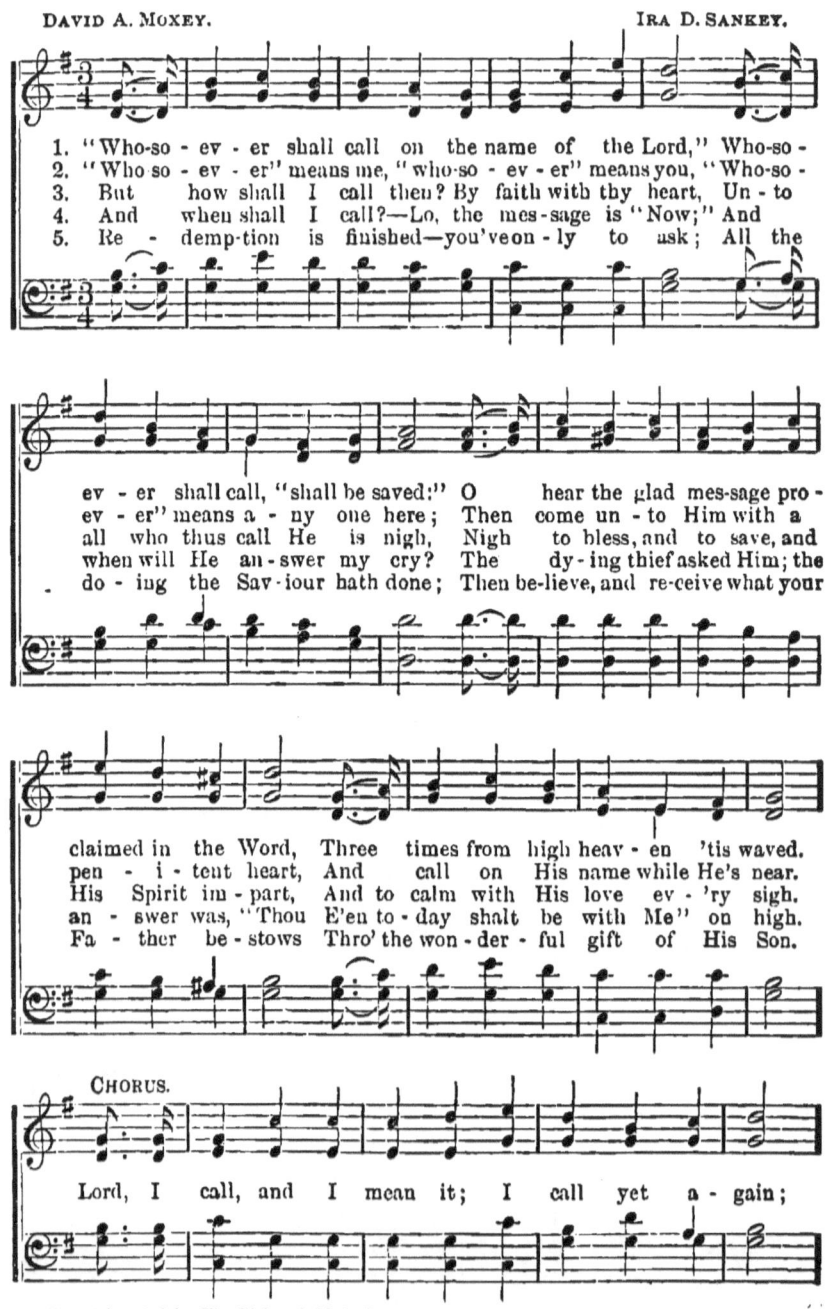

Whosoever Shall Call.—Concluded.

I confess Thee my Saviour and Lord; As I do so, I'm saved! *God says it;* Amen! I believe Him and rest on His word.

No. 92. Come, Holy Spirit, Come.

"Take not thy Holy Spirit from me."—Ps. 51: 11.

BENJ. BEDDOME.   LOWELL MASON.

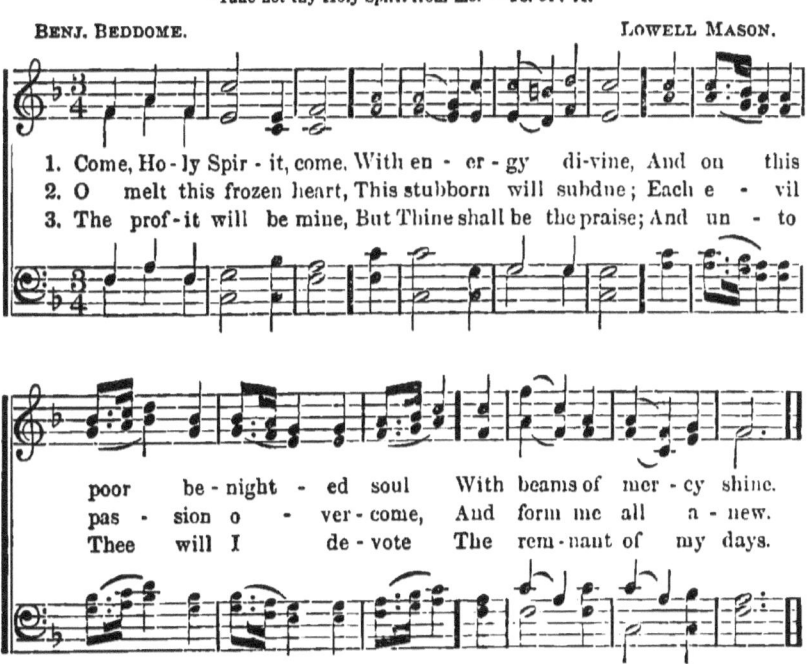

1. Come, Holy Spirit, come. With energy divine, And on this poor benighted soul With beams of mercy shine.
2. O melt this frozen heart, This stubborn will subdue; Each evil passion overcome, And form me all anew.
3. The profit will be mine, But Thine shall be the praise; And unto Thee will I devote The remnant of my days.

No. 93. No Friend Like Jesus.

"A friend that sticketh closer than a brother."—Prov. 18:24.

Mrs. C. E. Breck. D. B. Towner.

1. There is no friend like Je-sus, in weak-ness, No one who lifts such
2. There is no friend like Him in temp-ta-tion, Ful-ly He knows the
3. There is no friend like Je-sus, in sor-row; No one like Him hath
4. There is no friend such hope hath impart-ed; No one but Je-sus

bur-dens of care; No one like Him to strengthen and guide me,
depth of its power, Met it for me and triumphed for-ev-er,
sor-rowed and sighed; No one so com-forts me like a moth-er,
bring-eth such calm; No one who comes to earth's bro-ken heart-ed,

CHORUS.

No one like Him to heark-en to prayer.
Just to become my strength and my tower.
No one whose heart is o-pen so wide.
Ev-er bestows such heal-ing and balm.

There is no friend like Jesus my

Sav-iour, No one like Him to help and de-fend, No one like Him, my

Copyright, 1896, by D. B. Towner.

No Friend Like Jesus.—Concluded.

bless-ed Redeem-er, No one like Him, My won-der-ful Friend.

No. 94.   **Jesus is Mine.**

"My beloved is mine."—Songs of Solomon 2: 16.

H. J. M. Hope.   J. H. Burke.

1. Now   I have found a friend, Je-sus is mine; His love shall
2. When earth shall pass a-way, Je-sus is mine; In   the great
3. Fa-ther, Thy name I bless, Je-sus is mine; Thine was the

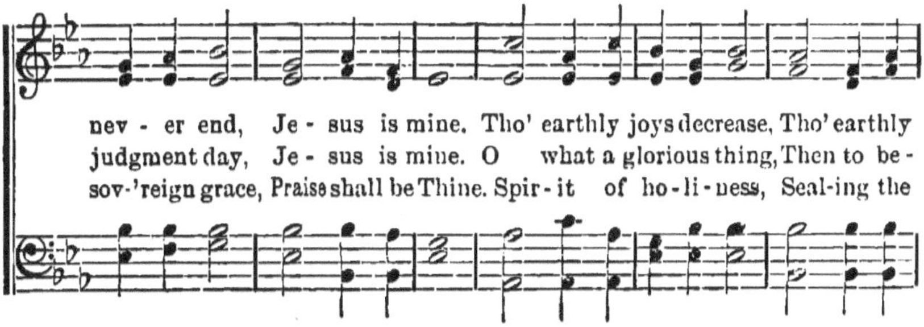

nev-er end, Je-sus is mine. Tho' earthly joys decrease, Tho' earthly
judgment day, Je-sus is mine. O what a glorious thing, Then to be-
sov-'reign grace, Praise shall be Thine. Spir-it of ho-li-ness, Seal-ing the

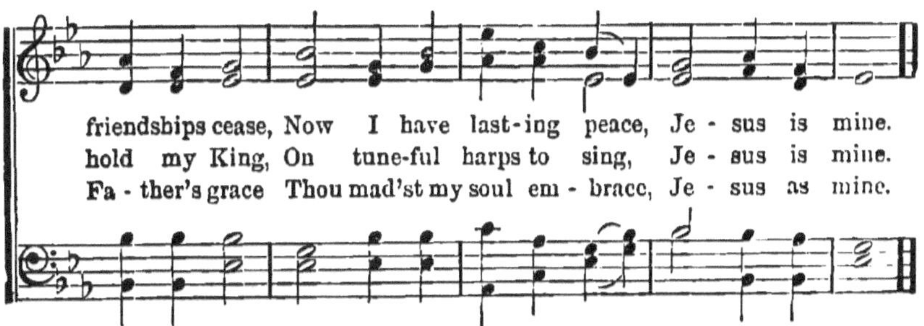

friendships cease, Now I have last-ing peace, Je-sus is mine.
hold my King, On   tune-ful harps to sing, Je-sus is mine.
Fa-ther's grace Thou mad'st my soul em-brace, Je-sus as mine.

Copyright, 1896, by The Biglow & Main Co.

No. 97. The Man of Galilee.

"For the Son of Man is come to seek and save that which was lost." Luke 19:10.

C. E. Breck. D. B. Towner.

1. A wondrous boon to man is giv'n, A gift of price-less worth,
   God's on-ly Son, the Prince of heav'n, To save the lost of earth.
   In low-li-ness He lived and wrought Deeds wonderful to see;
   And mul-ti-tudes with long-ing sought The Man of Gal-i-lee,

2. He came to break the liv-ing bread To starv-ing hu-man kind;
   To cleanse the lep-er, raise the dead, And heal the lame and blind;
   He came to reign where sin con-trols, To set the cap-tive free;
   Spake "Peace!" to waves and "Peace!" to souls, The Man of Gal-i-lee.

3. He came to show the heart of God, To give the wea-ry rest;
   And paths of deep-est sor-row trod, That sin-ners might be blest.
   He loved you since the world be-gan, He died to make you free;
   To be your Sav-iour, rose a-gain, The Christ of Gal-i-lee.

4. Oh, will you take His love di-vine? Choose now the bet-ter part,
   Let all His sav-ing grace be thine, And give to Him thy heart.
   His great com-pas-sion longs to bless,—Oh, heark-en to His plea,
   Make Him thy strength and righteousness, The Christ of Gal-i-lee.

Copyright, 1896, by D. B. Towner. Used by per.

The Man of Galilee.—Concluded.

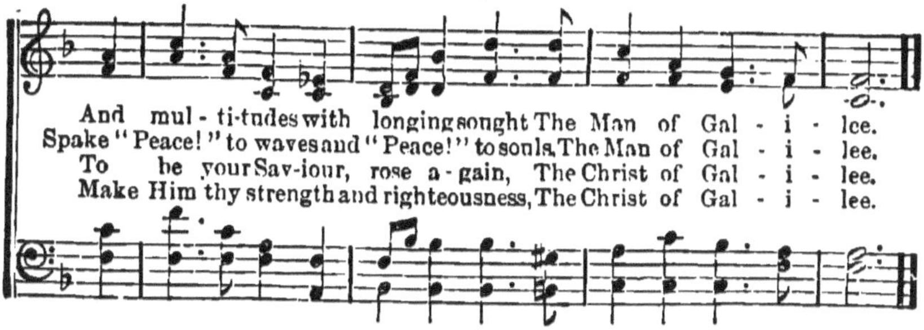

And mul-ti-tudes with longing sought The Man of Gal - i - lee.
Spake "Peace!" to waves and "Peace!" to souls, The Man of Gal - i - lee.
To be your Sav-iour, rose a-gain, The Christ of Gal - i - lee.
Make Him thy strength and righteousness, The Christ of Gal - i - lee.

No. 98. The Love of Jesus.

"The love of Christ constraineth us."—2 Cor. 5:14.

ROBERT BRUCE.   IRA D. SANKEY.

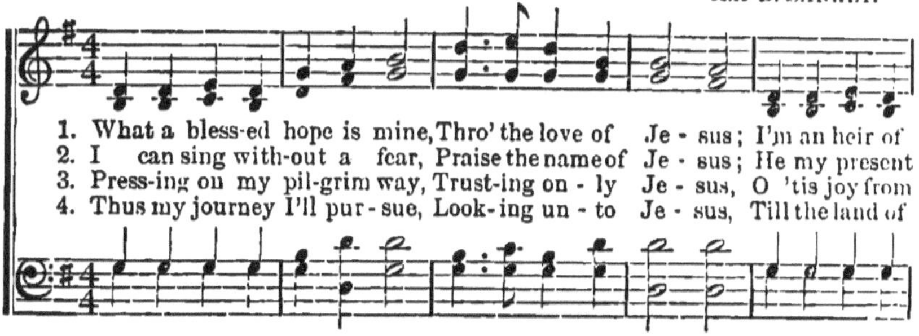

1. What a bless-ed hope is mine, Thro' the love of Je - sus; I'm an heir of
2. I can sing with-out a fear, Praise the name of Je - sus; He my present
3. Press-ing on my pil-grim way, Trust-ing on - ly Je - sus, O 'tis joy from
4. Thus my journey I'll pur-sue, Look-ing un - to Je - sus, Till the land of

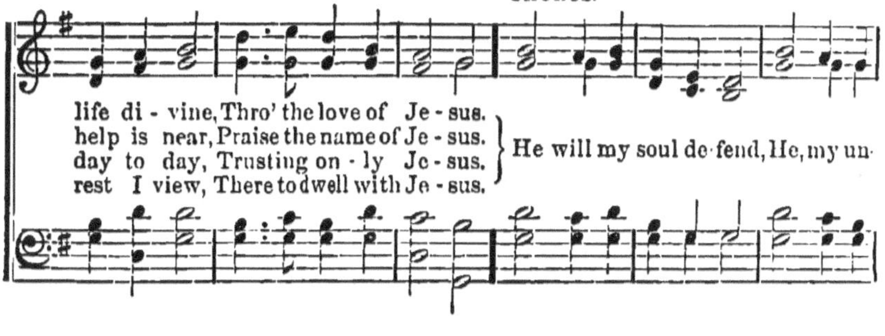

CHORUS.

life di-vine, Thro' the love of Je - sus.
help is near, Praise the name of Je - sus.
day to day, Trusting on - ly Je - sus.
rest I view, There to dwell with Je - sus.
} He will my soul de-fend, He, my un-

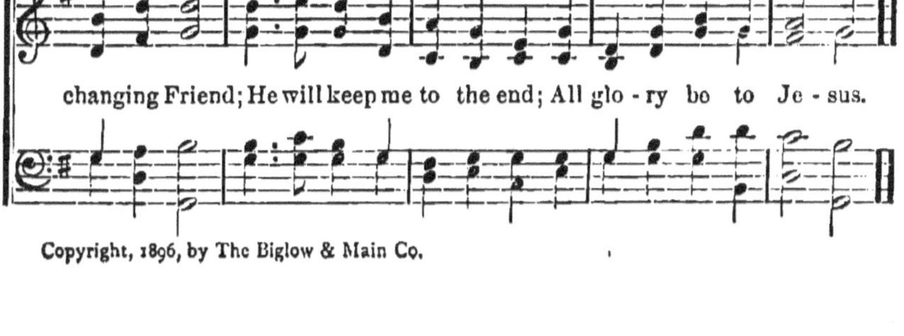

changing Friend; He will keep me to the end; All glo - ry be to Je - sus.

Copyright, 1896, by The Biglow & Main Co.

God is Love.—Concluded.

Tell it Again.—Concluded.

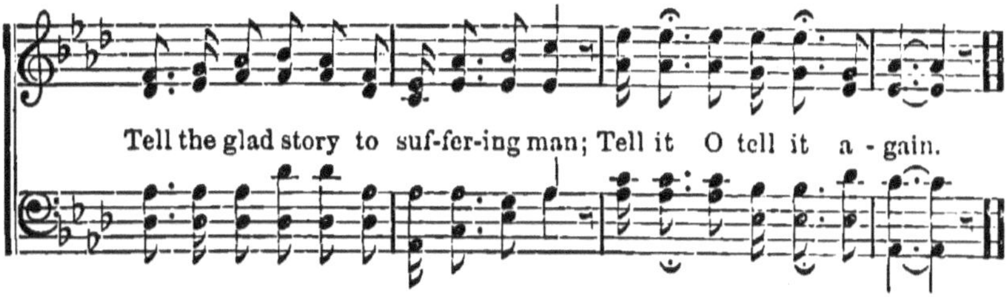

Tell the glad story to suf-fer-ing man; Tell it O tell it a - gain.

No. 101. Arise, Young Men, Arise.

"Put on the whole armor of God."—Eph. 6: 11.

Rev. J. H. Edwards.   Rev. Robert Lowry.

1. A-rise, young men, a-rise! Thy Sav-iour's lov-ing voice Now bids thee
2. A-rise! for death is nigh, Life's day is all too brief; Like light its
3. A-rise from dreams of fame, From sen-sual slum-ber rise; Keep spot-less

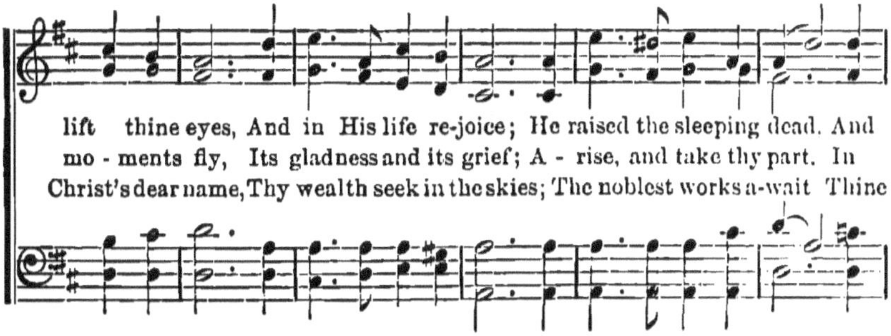

lift thine eyes, And in His life re-joice; He raised the sleeping dead. And
mo - ments fly, Its gladness and its grief; A - rise, and take thy part. In
Christ's dear name, Thy wealth seek in the skies; The noblest works a-wait Thine

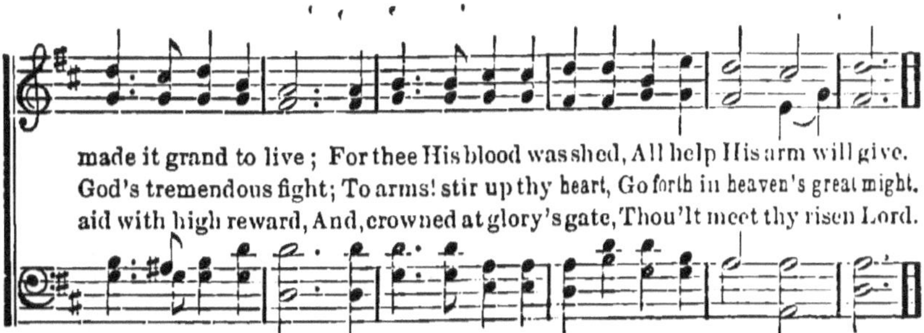

made it grand to live; For thee His blood was shed, All help His arm will give.
God's tremendous fight; To arms! stir up thy heart, Go forth in heaven's great might.
aid with high reward, And, crowned at glory's gate, Thou'lt meet thy risen Lord.

Copyright, 1886, by Biglow & Main.

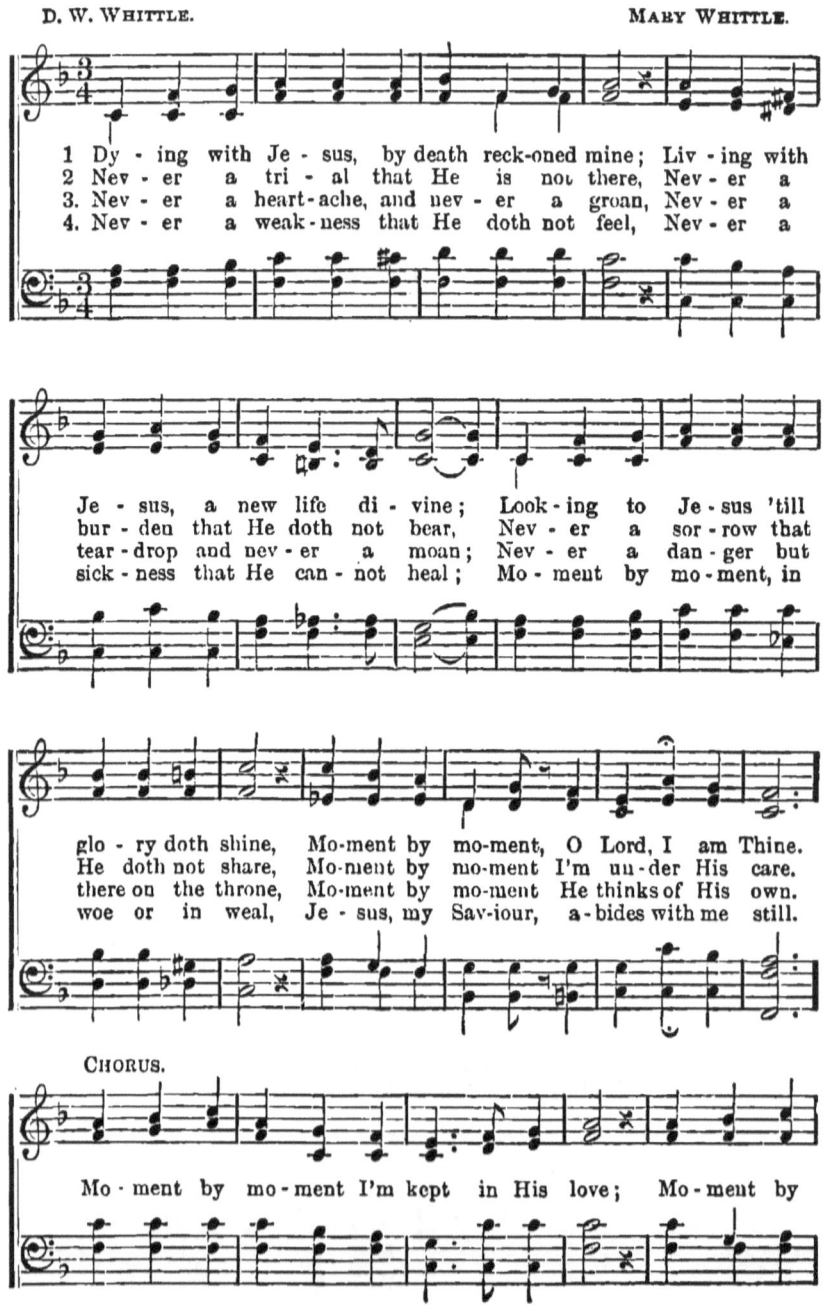

Moment by Moment.—Concluded.

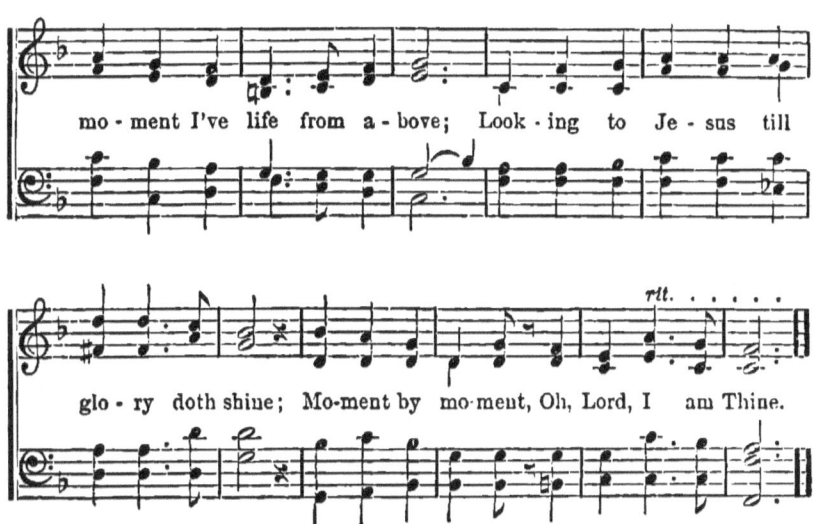

mo-ment I've life from a-bove; Look-ing to Je-sus till glo-ry doth shine; Mo-ment by mo-ment, Oh, Lord, I am Thine.

No. 103. Thou Art My Life.

"He that hath the Son hath life."—1 John 5: 12.

Rev. DWIGHT M. PRATT.   IRA D. SANKEY.

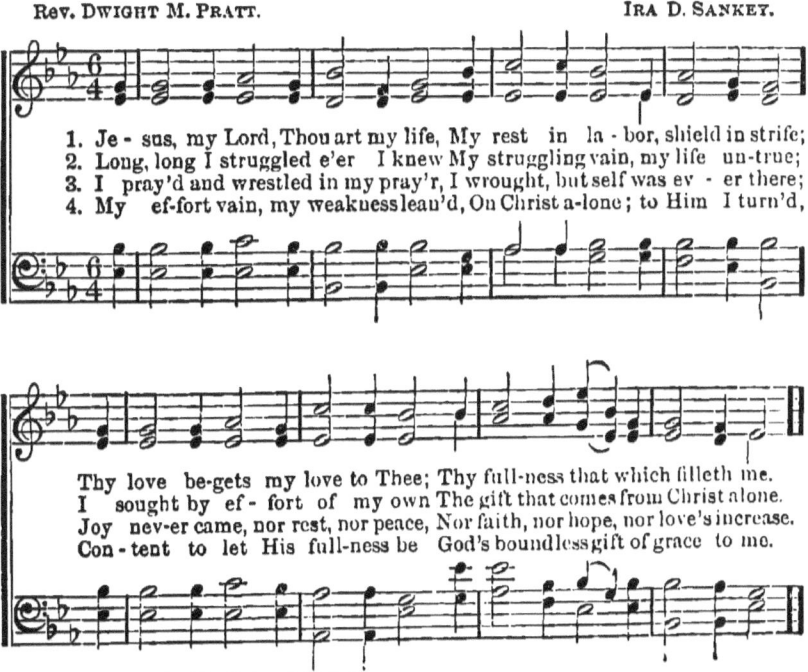

1. Je-sus, my Lord, Thou art my life, My rest in la-bor, shield in strife;
2. Long, long I struggled e'er I knew My struggling vain, my life un-true;
3. I pray'd and wrestled in my pray'r, I wrought, but self was ev-er there;
4. My ef-fort vain, my weakness lean'd, On Christ a-lone; to Him I turn'd,

Thy love be-gets my love to Thee; Thy full-ness that which filleth me.
I sought by ef-fort of my own The gift that comes from Christ alone.
Joy nev-er came, nor rest, nor peace, Nor faith, nor hope, nor love's increase.
Con-tent to let His full-ness be God's boundless gift of grace to me.

Copyright, 1896, by The Biglow & Main Co.

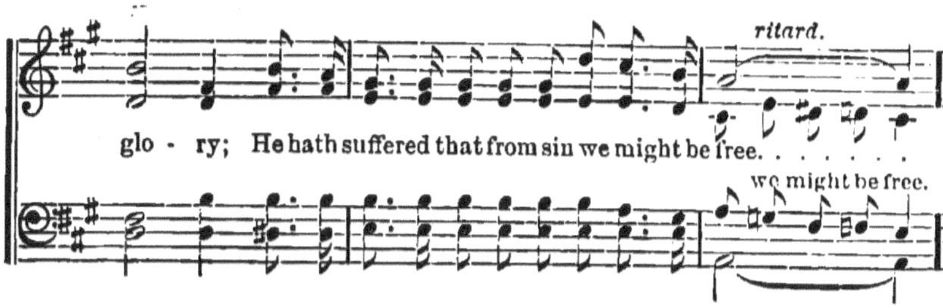

Let Us Sing Again.—Concluded.

ritard.

glo - ry; He hath suffered that from sin we might be free.......

we might be free.

No. 105. **God Heareth Prayer.**

"Hear my cry, O God; attend unto my prayer."—Ps. 61: 1.

Rev. R. F. Gordon.   Hubert P. Main.

1. Let not thy heart de-spair, Nor be a - fraid; God hear - eth
2. What tho' mis - for - tunes fall Part of thy lot; They can - not
3. This earth is not the home, Where thou shalt stay; Here con - stant

earn - est pray'r. He giv - eth aid; He is thy Help - er nigh,
take thine all, God chang-eth not; Look up with hope-ful glance,
chan - ges come, Time speeds a - way; Yet when life's transient gleam

And will thy need supply; Then on His love re - ly, Calm, undismayed.
Be of glad countenance; On - ward in faith advance, Sadness for - got.
Fades like a passing dream, Brightly on thee will beam An endless day.

Copyright, 1893, by The Biglow & Main Co.

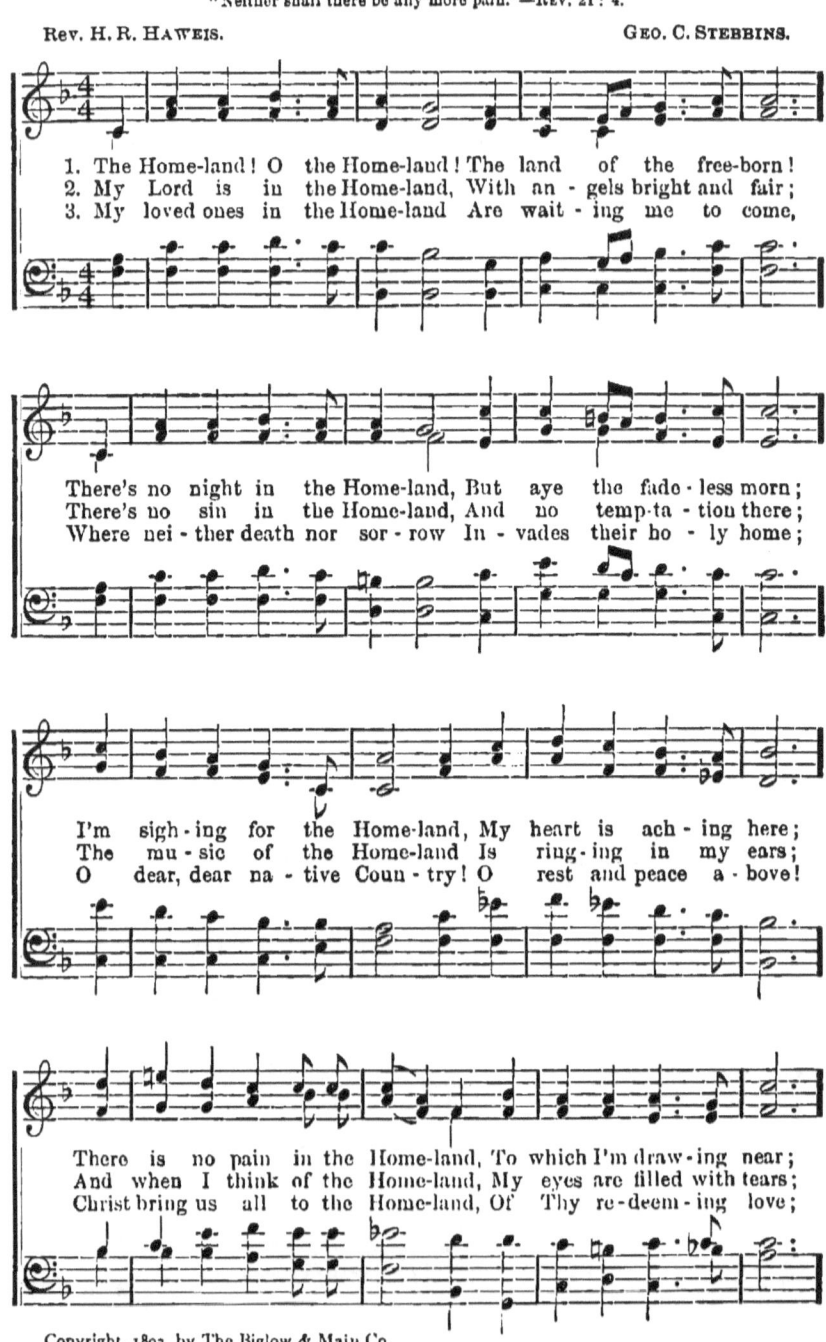

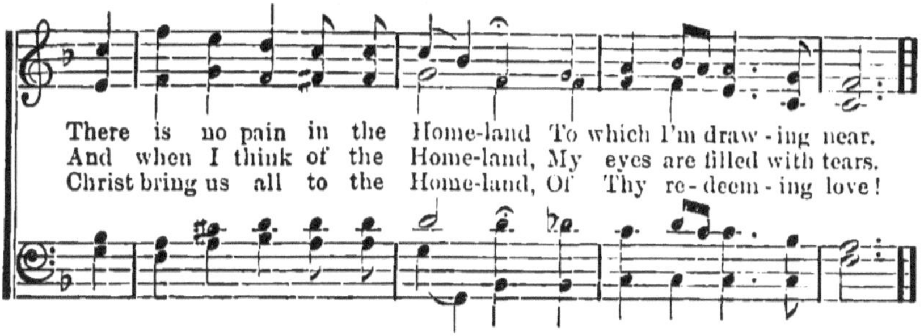

Homeland!—Concluded.

There is no pain in the Home-land To which I'm draw-ing near.
And when I think of the Home-land, My eyes are filled with tears.
Christ bring us all to the Home-land, Of Thy re-deem-ing love!

No. 109. One Sweetly Solemn Thought.

"Now they desire a better country that is, an heavenly."—Heb. 11: 16.

Miss PHOEBE CARY.   PHILIP PHILLIPS.

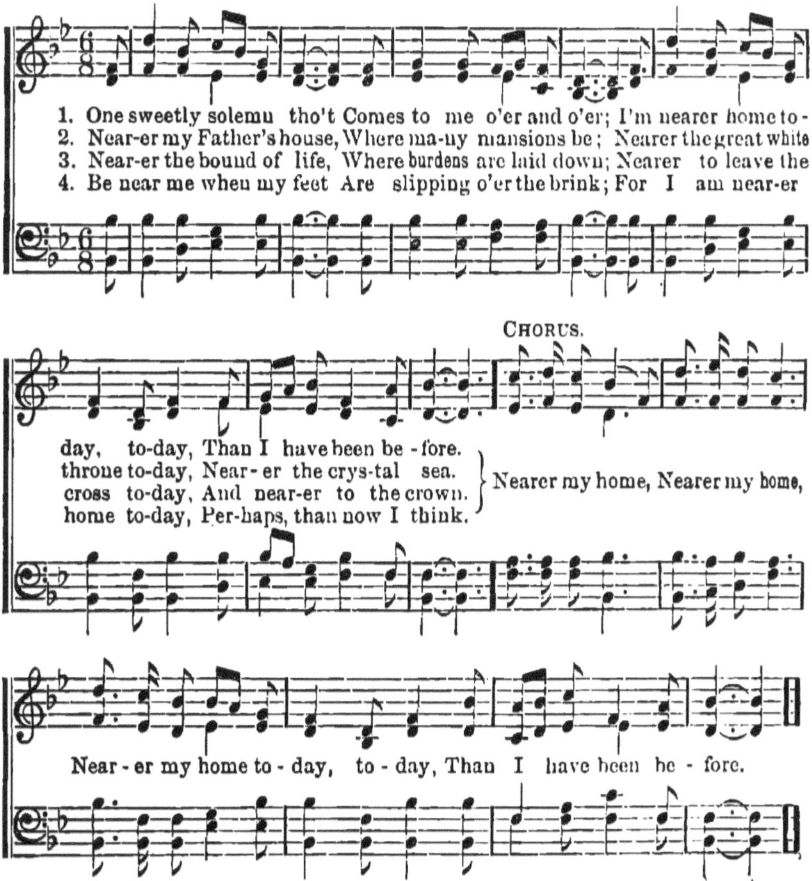

1. One sweetly solemn tho't Comes to me o'er and o'er; I'm nearer home to-
2. Near-er my Father's house, Where ma-ny mansions be; Nearer the great white
3. Near-er the bound of life, Where burdens are laid down; Nearer to leave the
4. Be near me when my feet Are slipping o'er the brink; For I am near-er

CHORUS.

day, to-day, Than I have been be-fore.
throne to-day, Near-er the crys-tal sea.
cross to-day, And near-er to the crown.
home to-day, Per-haps, than now I think.

Nearer my home, Nearer my home,

Near-er my home to-day, to-day, Than I have been be-fore.

Copyright property of The Biglow & Main Co.

No. 110. The Hope of the Coming of the Lord.

"Looking for that blessed hope."—TITUS 2: 13.

D. W. WHITTLE.
MAY WHITTLE MOODY.

1. A lamp in the night, a song in time of sor-row; A great glad hope which
2. A star in the sky, a beacon bright to guide us; An an-chor sure to
3. A call of command, like trumpet clearly sounding, To make us bold when
4. A word from the One to all our hearts the dear-est, A part-ing word to

faith can ev-er bor-row To gild the passing day with the glory of the morrow,
hold when storms betide us; A ref-uge for the soul, wherein quiet we may hide us,
e - vil is surrounding; To stir the sluggish heart, and to keep in good abounding,
make Him aye the near-est; Of all His precious words, the sweetest, brightest, clearest,

CHORUS. *Tempo.*

Is the hope of the coming of the Lord. Blessed hope, . . . blessed hope,
blessed hope, blessed hope,
Blessed hope of the coming of the Lord; How the aching heart it cheers,

Copyright, 1896, by May Whittle Moody.

The Hope of the Coming, etc.—Concluded.

How it glistens thro' our tears, Blessed hope of the coming of the Lord.

No. 111. Nothing But Leaves.

"He found nothing but leaves."—MARK 11:13.

L. E. AKERMAN, alt.   SILAS J. VAIL.

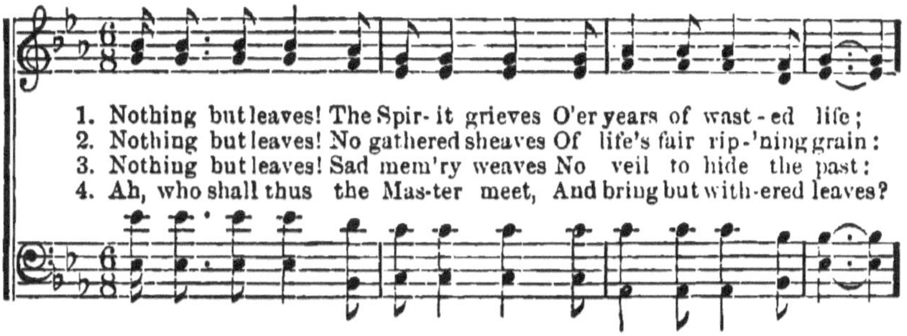

1. Nothing but leaves! The Spir-it grieves O'er years of wast-ed life;
2. Nothing but leaves! No gathered sheaves Of life's fair rip-'ning grain:
3. Nothing but leaves! Sad mem'ry weaves No veil to hide the past:
4. Ah, who shall thus the Mas-ter meet, And bring but with-ered leaves?

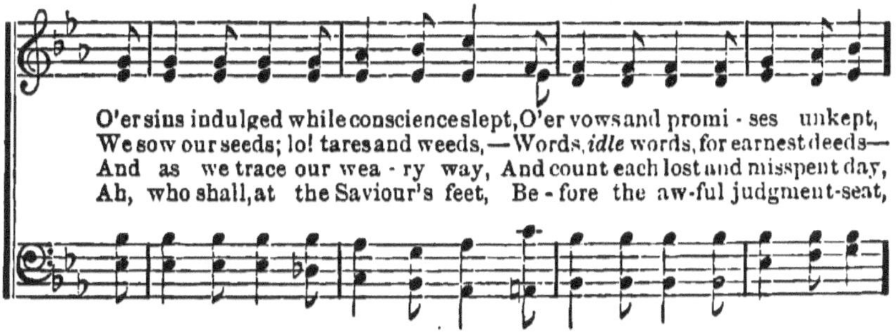

O'er sins indulged while conscience slept, O'er vows and promi-ses unkept,
We sow our seeds; lo! tares and weeds,—Words, *idle* words, for earnest deeds—
And as we trace our wea-ry way, And count each lost and misspent day,
Ah, who shall, at the Saviour's feet, Be-fore the aw-ful judgment-seat,

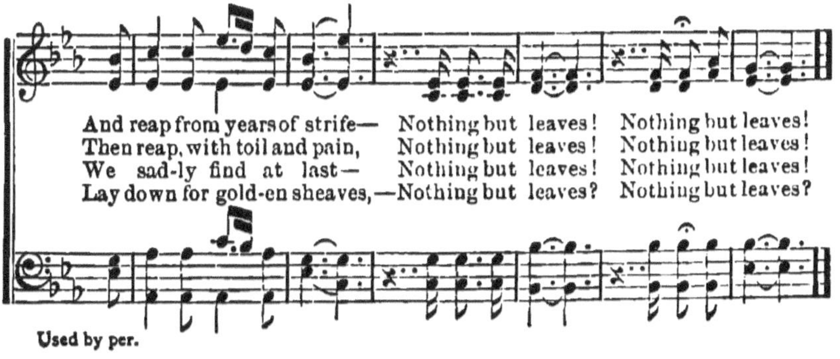

And reap from years of strife— Nothing but leaves! Nothing but leaves!
Then reap, with toil and pain, Nothing but leaves! Nothing but leaves!
We sad-ly find at last— Nothing but leaves! Nothing but leaves!
Lay down for gold-en sheaves,—Nothing but leaves? Nothing but leaves?

Used by per.

No. 112. Loyalty to Christ.

"Whatsoever he saith unto you, do it."—JOHN 2: 5.

Dr. E. T. CASSELL.   FLORA H. CASSELL.

1. Up - on the western plain There comes the sig-nal strain, 'Tis loy-al-ty,
2. O hear ye brave the sound That moves the earth a-round, 'Tis loy-al-ty,
3. Come, join our loy-al throng, We'll rout the gi-ant wrong, 'Tis loy-al-ty,
4. The strength of youth we lay At Je-sus' feet to - day, 'Tis loy-al-ty,

loy - al - ty, loy - al - ty to Christ; Its mu-sic rolls a - long, The
loy - al - ty, loy - al - ty to Christ; A - rise to dare and do, Ring
loy - al - ty, loy - al - ty to Christ; Where Sa-tan's ban - ners float, We'll
loy - al - ty, loy - al - ty to Christ; His gos - pel we'll pro-claim, Thro'

hills take up the song, Of loy-al-ty, loy-al-ty, Yes, loy-al-ty to Christ.
out the watch-word true, Of loy-al-ty, loy-al-ty, Yes, loy-al-ty to Christ.
send this bu - gle note, Of loy-al-ty, loy-al-ty, Yes, loy-al-ty to Christ.
out the world's do-main, Of loy-al-ty, loy-al-ty, Yes, loy-al-ty to Christ.

CHORUS.

"On to vic - to - ry! On to vic - to - ry!" Cries our great Commander;
"On!" . . . . . . We'll move at His command, We'll soon possess the
great Com-man-der, "On!"

Copyright, 1894, by E. O. Excell. Used by per.

Loyalty to Christ.—Concluded.

land, Thro' loy-al-ty, loy-al-ty, Yes, loy-al-ty to Christ.

No. 113. Saved to Serve.

"Serve the Lord with gladness."—Psa. 100: 2.

EL NATHAN. JAMES McGRANAHAN.

1. Go - ing forth at Christ's command, Go - ing forth to ev - 'ry land;
2. Serv-ing God through all our days, Toil-ing not for purse or praise;
3. Seek-ing on - ly souls to win, From the dead - ly pow'r of sin;

Full sal - va - tion making known, Thro' the blood of God's dear Son.
But to mag - ni - fy His name, While the gos - pel we pro - claim.
We would guide their steps a - right, Out of dark-ness in - to light.

CHORUS.

"Saved to serve!" the watch-word ring, Saved to serve our glo-rious King;

Tell the sto - ry o'er and o'er Saved to serve for - ev - er - more.

Copyright, 1895, by James McGranahan.

When the Saints are Marching in.—Concluded.

No. 115. I'll Live for Thee.

"Whether we live therefore, or die, we are the Lord's."—Rom. 14: 8.

R. E. Hudson.   C. R. Dunbar.

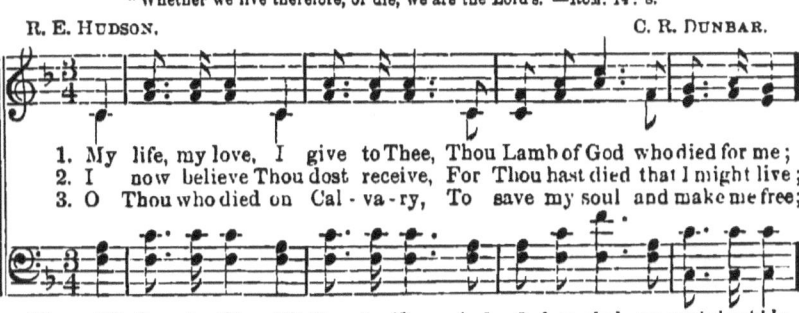

1. My life, my love, I give to Thee, Thou Lamb of God who died for me;
2. I now believe Thou dost receive, For Thou hast died that I might live;
3. O Thou who died on Cal-va-ry, To save my soul and make me free;

Cho.—I'll live for Thee, I'll live for Thee, And O how glad my soul should be,

D.C. for Cho.

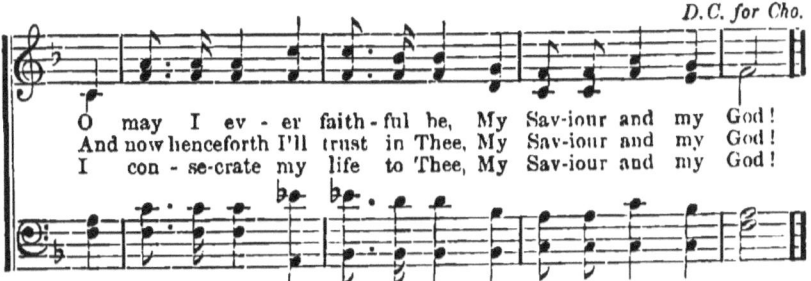

O may I ev - er faith-ful be, My Sav-iour and my God!
And now henceforth I'll trust in Thee, My Sav-iour and my God!
I con - se-crate my life to Thee, My Sav-iour and my God!

That Thou didst give Thy - self for me, My Sav-iour and my God!

Copyright, 1882, by R. E. Hudson. Used by per.

He Saves Me.—Concluded.

CHORUS.

taught me, And made my heart per-fect-ly whole.
dore Him, Re-stored to His lov-ing em-brace. } He saves me, He
know-ing, That Je-sus the Sav-iour is mine.

saves me, His love fills my soul, halle-lu-jah! Oh, glo-ry, He saves me,

1. His spir-it a-bid-eth with-in;
2. His blood cleanseth me from all sin.

No. 117. Grace, before and after Meat.

(Rockingham. L. M.)

JOHN CENNICK.   LOWELL MASON.

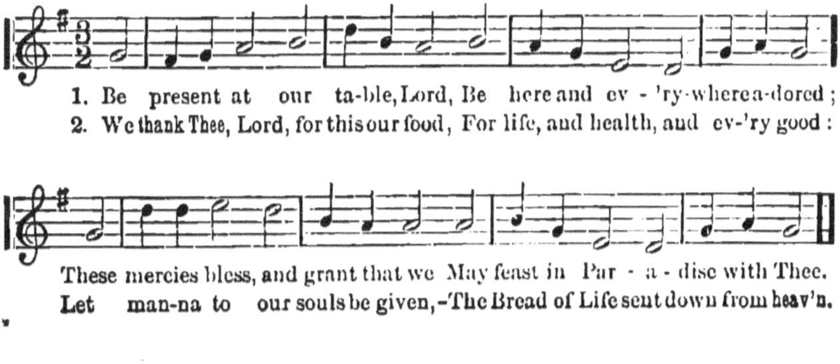

1. Be present at our ta-ble, Lord, Be here and ev-'ry-where a-dored;
2. We thank Thee, Lord, for this our food, For life, and health, and ev-'ry good:

These mercies bless, and grant that we May feast in Par-a-dise with Thee.
Let man-na to our souls be given,—The Bread of Life sent down from heav'n.

Saved by Grace.—Concluded.

face, And tell the sto-ry— Saved by grace.
to face,

No. 119. "Not I, but Christ."

"Not I, but Christ liveth in me." GAL. 2: 20.

A. A. F. J. H. BURKE.

1. "Not I, but Christ," be honored, loved, ex-alt-ed; "Not I, but
2. "Not I, but Christ," to gent-ly soothe in sor-row; "Not I, but
3. "Not I, but Christ," in low-ly, si-lent la bor; "No I, but
4. Christ, on-ly Christ, ere long will fill my vis-ion; Glo-ry ex-

Christ," be seen, be known, be heard; "Not I, but Christ," in ev-'ry look and
Christ," to wipe the falling tear: "Not I, but Christ," to lift the wear-y
Christ," in humble, earnest toil: Christ, only Christ! no show, no os-ten-
cell-ing soon, full soon I'll see— Christ, only Christ, my ev-'ry wish ful-

ac-tion, "Not I, but Christ," in ev-'ry thought and word.
bur-den; "Not I, but Christ," to hush a-way all fear.
ta-tion; Christ, none but Christ the gath'r-er of the spoil.
fill-ing—Christ, on-ly Christ, my All in All to be.

Copyright, 1896, by The Biglow & Main Co.

There is Never a Day.—Concluded.

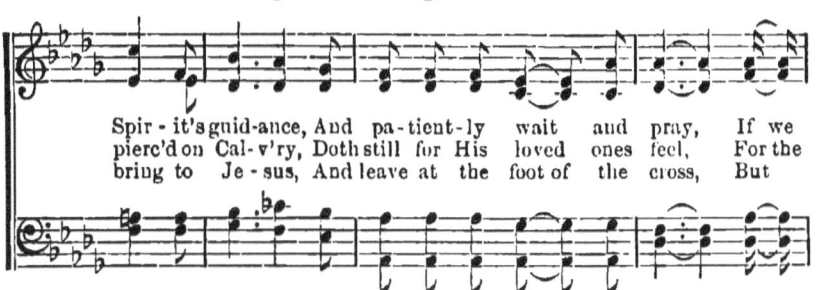

Spir-it's guid-ance, And pa-tient-ly wait and pray, If we
pierc'd on Cal-v'ry, Doth still for His loved ones feel, For the
bring to Je-sus, And leave at the foot of the cross, But

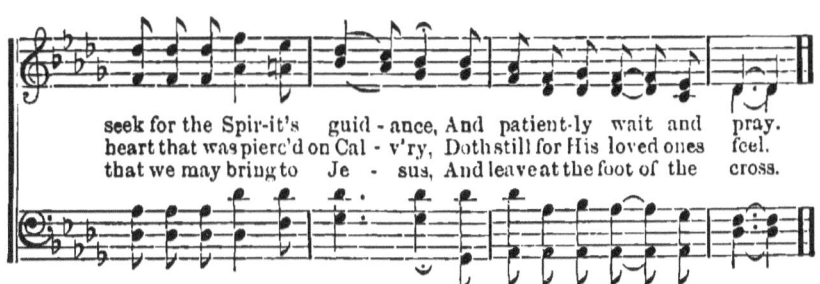

seek for the Spir-it's guid-ance, And patient-ly wait and pray.
heart that was pierc'd on Cal-v'ry, Doth still for His loved ones feel.
that we may bring to Je-sus, And leave at the foot of the cross.

No. 123. Praise God from Whom.

(Old Hundred. L. M.)

Rev. THOMAS KEN. L. BOURGEOIS.

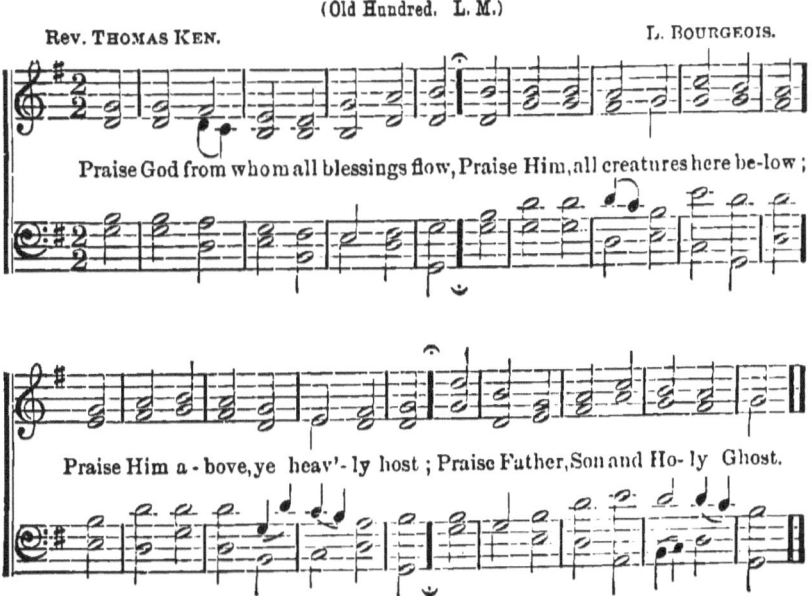

Praise God from whom all blessings flow, Praise Him, all creatures here be-low;

Praise Him a-bove, ye heav'-ly host; Praise Father, Son and Ho-ly Ghost.

Awake, Awake, etc.—Concluded.

No. 125. There is a Green Hill far away.

CECIL F. ALEXANDER. GEO. C. STEBBINS.

Moderato.

1. There is a green hill far a-way, Without a cit-y wall; Where the dear Lord was
2. We may not know, we can-not tell What pains He had to bear; But we be-lieve it
3. He died that we might be forgiven, He died to make us good, That we might go at
4. There was no oth-er good enough, To pay the price of sin; He on-ly could un-

CHORUS.

cru-ci-fied, Who died to save us all.
was for us, He hung and suf-fered there.
last to heav'n, Sav'd by His pre-cious blood.
lock the gate Of heav'n and let us in.

Oh, dear-ly, dear-ly has He loved, And

rit.

we must love Him too; And trust in His re-deem-ing blood, And try His works to do.

Copyright, 1878, by Geo. C. Stebbins. Used by per.

Faith is the Victory.—Concluded.

Oh, glo-ri-ous vic-to-ry, That o-ver-comes the world.

No. 129. Our Saviour King.

J. H. JOHNSTON. JAMES McGRANAHAN.

1. He lives and loves, our Sav-iour King; With joy-ful lips your trib-ute bring;
2. His Hand is strong, His word en-dures, His sac-ri-fice our peace se-cures;
3. Each day re-veals His con-stant love, With "mer-cies new" from heav'n a-bove;

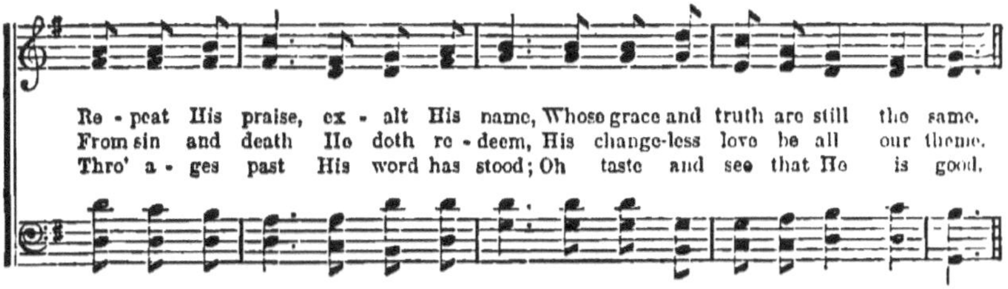

Re-peat His praise, ex-alt His name, Whose grace and truth are still the same.
From sin and death He doth re-deem, His change-less love be all our theme.
Thro' a-ges past His word has stood; Oh taste and see that He is good.

CHORUS.

His mer-cy flows, an end-less stream, To all e-ter-ni-ty the same,

To all e-ter-ni-ty, to all e-ter-ni-ty, To all e-ter-ni-ty the same.

Copyright, 1891, by James McGranahan. All rights reserved.

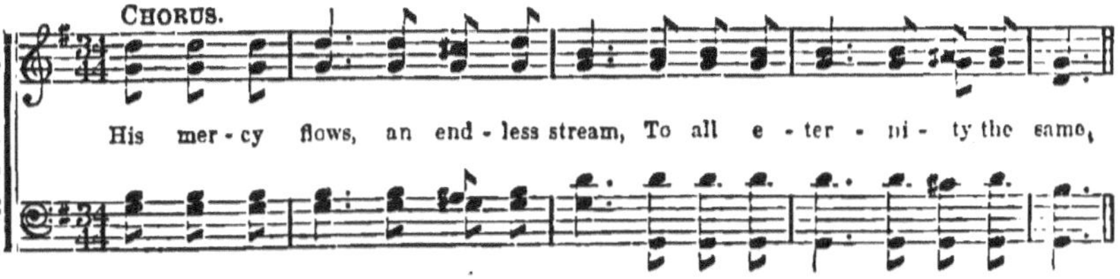

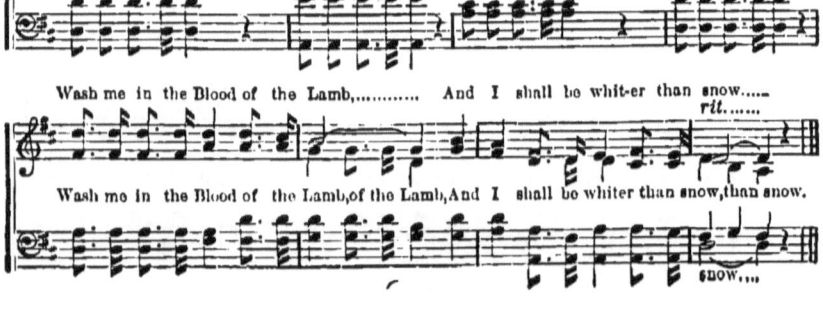

Hear us, O Saviour.—Concluded.

No. 134. **What a Wonderful Saviour!**

E. A. H. ELISHA A. HOFFMAN.

1. Christ has for sin a-tone-ment made, What a won-der-ful Sav-iour! We
2. I praise Him for the cleans-ing blood, What a won-der-ful Sav-iour! That
3. He cleansed my heart from all its sin, What a won-der-ful Sav-iour! And
4. He walks be-side me all the way, What a won-der-ful Sav-iour! And

are redeemed! the price is paid! What a won-der-ful Sav-iour!
rec-on-ciled my soul to God; What a won-der-ful Sav-iour!
now He reigns and rules there-in; What a won-der-ful Sav-iour!
keeps me faith-ful day by day; What a won-der-ful Sav-iour!

CHORUS.

What a won-der-ful Sav-iour is Je-sus, my Je-sus! What a won-der-ful Sav-iour is Je-sus, my Lord!

5 He gives me overcoming power,
  What a wonderful Saviour!
And triumph in each trying hour;
  What a wonderful Saviour!

6 To Him I've given all my heart,
  What a wonderful Saviour!
The world shall never share a part;
  What a wonderful Saviour!

No. 135. Come, Thou Almighty King.

CHARLES WESLEY. (Italian Hymn. 6s, 4s.) FELICE GIARDINI.

1. Come, Thou al-might-y King, Help us Thy name to sing, Help us to praise: Fa-ther! all-
2. Come, Thou in-car-nate Word, Gird on Thy might-y sword; Our pray'r at-tend: Come, and Thy
3. Come, ho-ly Com-fort-er! Thy sa-cred wit-ness bear, In this glad hour: Thou, who al-
4. To the great One in Three, The highest prais-es be, Hence ev-er-more! His sov'reign

glo-ri-ous, O'er all vic-to-ri-ous, Come, and reign o-ver us, An-cient of Days!
peo-ple bless, And give Thy word suc-cess: Spir-it of ho-li-ness! On us de-scend.
might-y art, Now rule in ev-'ry heart, And ne'er from us de-part, Spir-it of pow'r!
maj-es-ty May we in glo-ry see, And to e-ter-ni-ty Love and a-dore.

No. 136. Speed Away.

F. J. CROSBY. I. B. WOODBURY, arr.

1. Speed a-way, speed a-way on your mis-sion of light, To the lands that are
2. Speed a-way, speed a-way with the life-giv-ing Word, To the na-tions that
3. Speed a-way, speed a-way with the mes-sage of rest, To the souls by the

ly-ing in dark-ness and night, 'Tis the Mas-ter's com-mand; go ye forth in His
know not the voice of the Lord; Take the wings of the morn-ing and fly o'er the
tempt-er in bond-age op-press'd; For the Sav-iour has pur-chas'd their ran-som from

name, The won-der-ful Gos-pel of Je-sus pro-claim; Take your lives in your
wave, In the strength of your Mas-ter the lost ones to save; He is call-ing once
sin; And the ban-quet is read-y, O gath-er them in; To the res-cue make

Words and Har. Copyright, 1890, by Ira D. Sankey.

Speed Away.—Concluded.

hand, to the work while 'tis day,
more, not a mo-ment's de-lay, } Speed a-way, speed a-way, speed a-way.
haste, there's no time for de-lay,

No. 137. A Soldier of the Cross.

ISAAC WATTS.   IRA D. SANKEY.

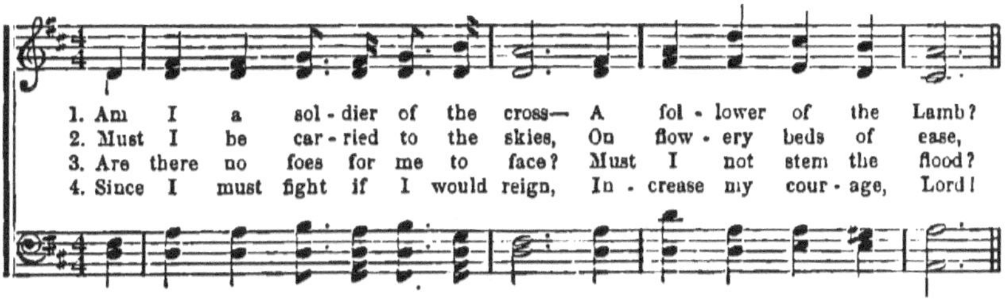

1. Am I a sol-dier of the cross— A fol-lower of the Lamb?
2. Must I be car-ried to the skies, On flow-ery beds of ease,
3. Are there no foes for me to face? Must I not stem the flood?
4. Since I must fight if I would reign, In-crease my cour-age, Lord!

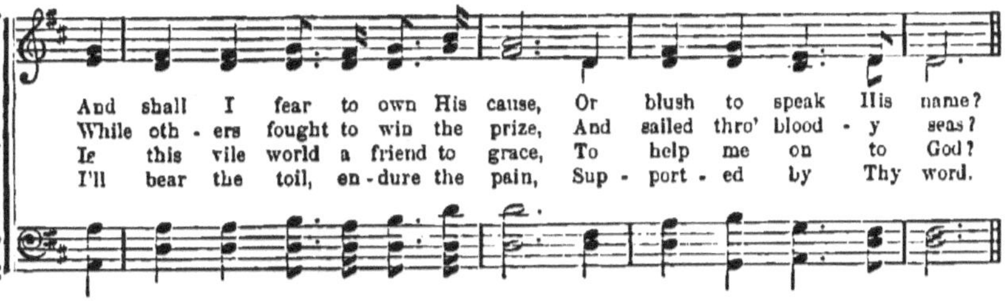

And shall I fear to own His cause, Or blush to speak His name?
While oth-ers fought to win the prize, And sailed thro' blood-y seas?
Is this vile world a friend to grace, To help me on to God?
I'll bear the toil, en-dure the pain, Sup-port-ed by Thy word.

Copyright, 1880, by Ira D. Sankey.

CHORUS.

In the name............ of Christ the King, Who hath
In the name   of Christ the King,

purchas'd life for me, Thro' grace I'll win the promised crown, What-e'er my cross may be.

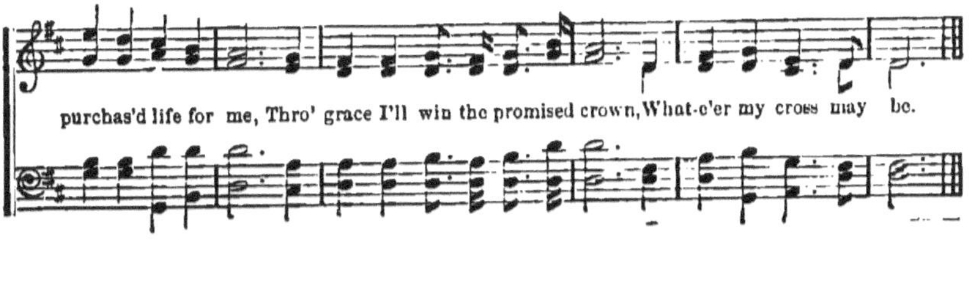

When the Mists, etc.—Concluded.

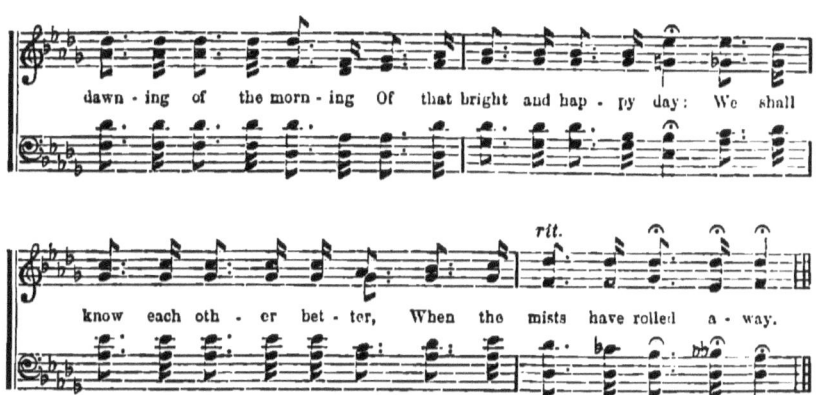

No. 139. Sweet Hour of Prayer.

W. W. WALFORD. WM. B. BRADBURY.

2 Sweet hour of prayer! sweet hour of prayer!
Thy wings shall my petition bear
To Him whose truth and faithfulness
Engage the waiting soul to bless;
And since He bids me seek His face,
Believe His word, and trust His grace,
|: I'll cast on Him my every care,
And wait for thee, sweet hour of prayer! :|

3 Sweet hour of prayer! sweet hour of prayer!
May I thy consolation share,
Till, from Mount Pisgah's lofty height,
I view my home and take my flight;
This robe of flesh I'll drop, and rise
To seize the everlasting prize;
|: And shout, while passing through the air,
Farewell, farewell, sweet hour of prayer! :|

No. 140. What a Friend We have in Jesus.

JOSEPH SCRIVEN. Alt. CHARLES C. CONVERSE.

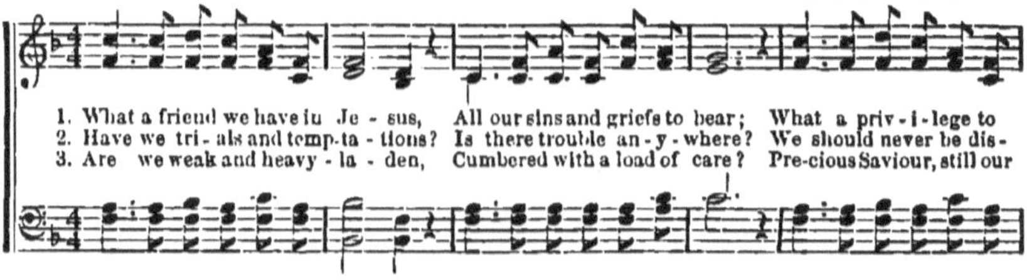

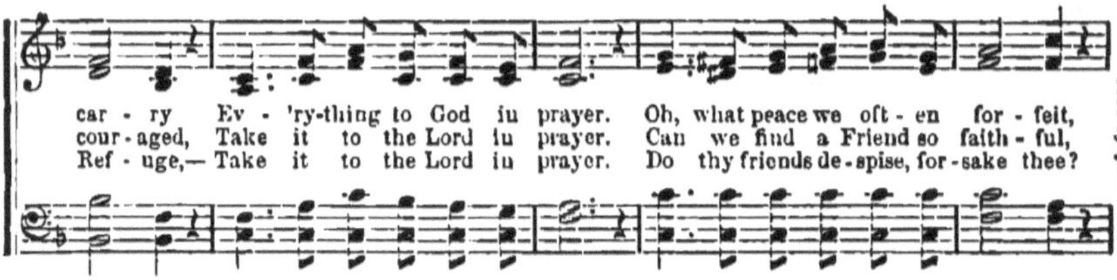

Used by per.

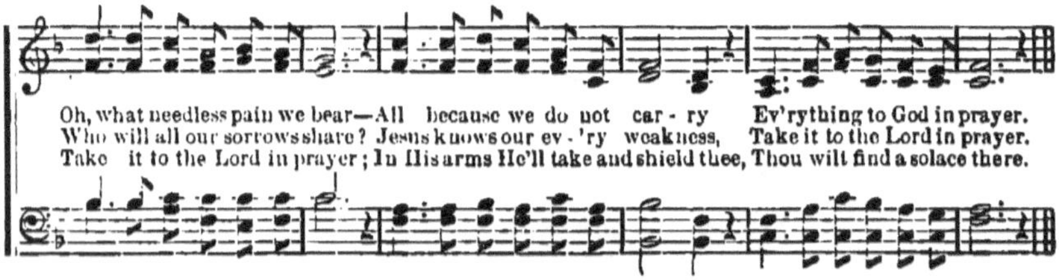

No. 141. Holy, Holy! Lord God Almighty!

REGINALD HEBER, D.D. Rev. JOHN B. DYKES.

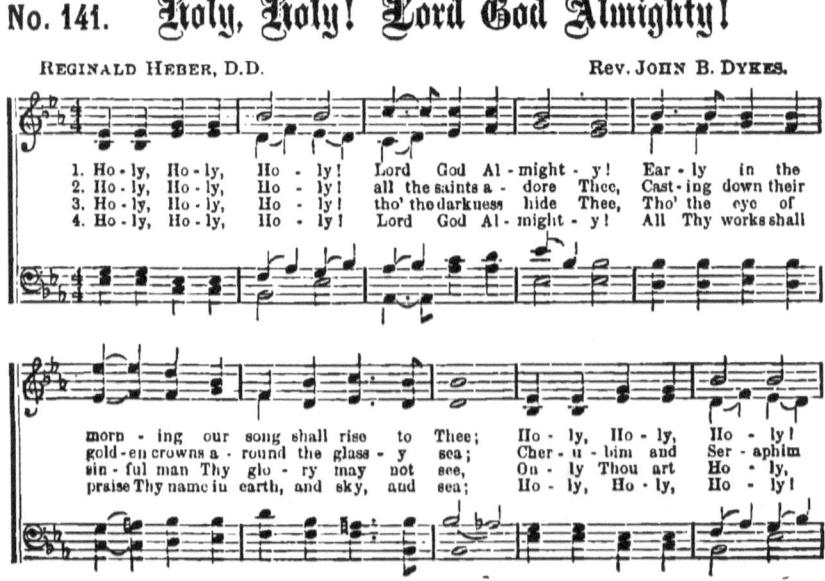

Holy, Holy! Lord, etc.—Concluded.

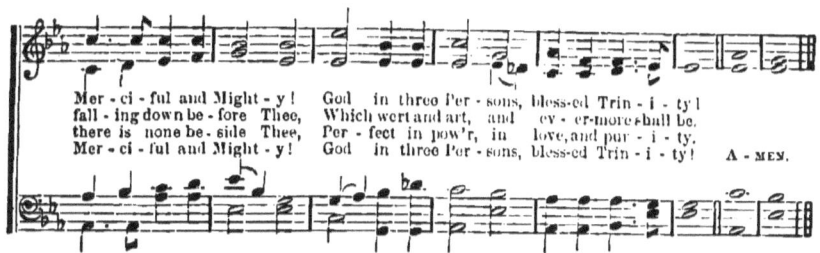

Mer - ci - ful and Might - y! God in three Per - sons, bless-ed Trin - i - ty!
fall - ing down be - fore Thee, Which wert and art, and ev - er-more shall be.
there is none be - side Thee, Per - fect in pow'r, in love, and pur - i - ty.
Mer - ci - ful and Might - y! God in three Per - sons, bless-ed Trin - i - ty! A - MEN.

No. 142. Shall you? Shall I?

G. M. J. (Subject from M. E. I.) JAMES McGRANAHAN.

1. Some one will en - ter the pearl - y gate By and by, by and by,
2. Some one will glad - ly his cross lay down By and by, by and by,
3. Some one will knock when the door is shut By and by, by and by,
4. Some one will sing the tri - umph - ant song By and by, by and by,

Repeat pp.

Taste of the glo - ries that there a - wait, Shall you? shall I?........
Faith-ful, ap-proved, shall re - ceive a crown, Shall you? shall I?........
Hear a voice say - ing, "I know you not," Shall you? shall I?........
Join in the praise with the blood - bought throng, Shall you? shall I?........

Some one will trav - el the streets of gold, Beau - ti - ful vis - ions will
Some one the glo - ri - ous King will see, Ev - er from sor - row of
Some one will call and shall not be heard, Vain - ly will strive when the
Some one will greet on the gold - en shore, Loved ones of earth who have

Repeat pp.

there be - hold, Feast on the pleasures so long fore-told: Shall you? shall I?........
earth be free, Hap - py with Him thro' e - ter - ni - ty; Shall you? shall I?........
door is barred, Someone will fail of the saint's re-ward: Shall you? shall I?........
gone be - fore, Safe in the glo - ry for ev - er-more: Shall you? shall I?........

Copyright, 1887, by James McGranahan.

No. 143. God be With You!

J. E. RANKIN.   W. G. TOMER.

1. God be with you till we meet a-gain!—By His coun-sels guide, up-hold you,
2. God be with you till we meet a-gain!—'Neath His wings pro-tect-ing hide you,
3. God be with you till we meet a-gain!—When life's per-ils thick con-found you,
4. God be with you till we meet a-gain!—Keep love's ban-ner float-ing o'er you,

With His sheep se-cure-ly fold you; God be with you till we meet a-gain!
Dai-ly man-na still di-vide you; God be with you till we meet a-gain!
Put His arms un-fail-ing round you; God be with you till we meet a-gain!
Smite death's threat'ning wave before you; God be with you till we meet a-gain!

By per. of J. E. Rankin.

CHORUS.

Till we meet!......... Till we meet! Till we meet at Je-sus' feet;
Till we meet! Till we meet a-gain!   Till we meet!

Till we meet!......... Till we meet! God be with you till we meet a-gain!
Till we meet! Till we meet a-gain!

No. 144. My Jesus, as Thou Wilt.

JANE BORTHWICK, tr.   (Jewett. 6s. D.)   WEBER, arr. by H. P. MAIN.

1. My Je-sus, as Thou wilt; Oh, may Thy will be mine;
2. My Je-sus, as Thou wilt; Tho' seen thro' many a tear,
3. My Je-sus, as Thou wilt; All shall be well for me;

My Jesus, as Thou Wilt.—Concluded.

In - to Thy hand of love I would my all re - sign;
Let not my star of hope Grow dim or dis - ap - pear;
Each chang-ing fu - ture scene I glad - ly trust with Thee:

Thro' sor - row or thro' joy, Con - duct me as Thine own,
Since Thou on earth hast wept, And sor - rowed oft a - lone,
Straight to my home a - bove I trav - el calm - ly on,

Rit.

And help me still to say, My Lord, Thy will be done.
If I must weep with Thee, My Lord, Thy will be done.
And sing, in life or death,— My Lord, Thy will be done.

No. 145. Holy Ghost, with Light Divine.

(Mercy. 7s.)

ANDREW REED.   GOTTSCHALK, arr. by H. P. MAIN.

1. Ho - ly Ghost, with light di - vine, Shine up - on this heart of mine;
2. Ho - ly Ghost, with pow'r di - vine, Cleanse this guilt - y heart of mine;
3. Ho - ly Ghost, with joy di - vine, Cheer this sad - dened heart of mine;
4. Ho - ly Spir - it, all di - vine, Dwell with-in this heart of mine;

Chase the shades of night a - way, Turn my dark - ness in - to day.
Long hath sin, with - out con - trol, Held do - min - ion o'er my soul.
Bid my ma - ny woes de - part, Heal my wound-ed, bleed-ing heart.
Cast down ev - 'ry i - dol throne, Reign su - preme—and reign a - lone.

By per. O. Ditson Co., owners of copyright.

No. 146. More Love to Thee, O Christ.

Mrs. ELIZABETH PRENTISS. W. H. DOANE.

1. More love to Thee, O Christ! More love to Thee; Hear Thou the pray'r I make On bend-ed knee; This is my earn-est plea, More love, O Christ, to Thee, More love to Thee! More love to Thee!
2. Once earth-ly joy I craved, Sought peace and rest; Now Thee a-lone I seek, Give what is best; This all my pray'r shall be,
3. Let sor-row do its work, Come grief or pain; Sweet are Thy mes-sen-gers, Sweet their re-frain, When they can sing with me,—
4. Then shall my lat-est breath, Whis-per Thy praise, This be the part-ing cry My heart shall raise; This still its pray'r shall be:

Copyright property of The Biglow & Main Co.

No. 147. Throw out the Life-Line.

(May be sung as a Solo and Chorus.)

Rev. E. S. UFFORD. E. S. UFFORD. Arr. by GEO. C. STEBBINS.

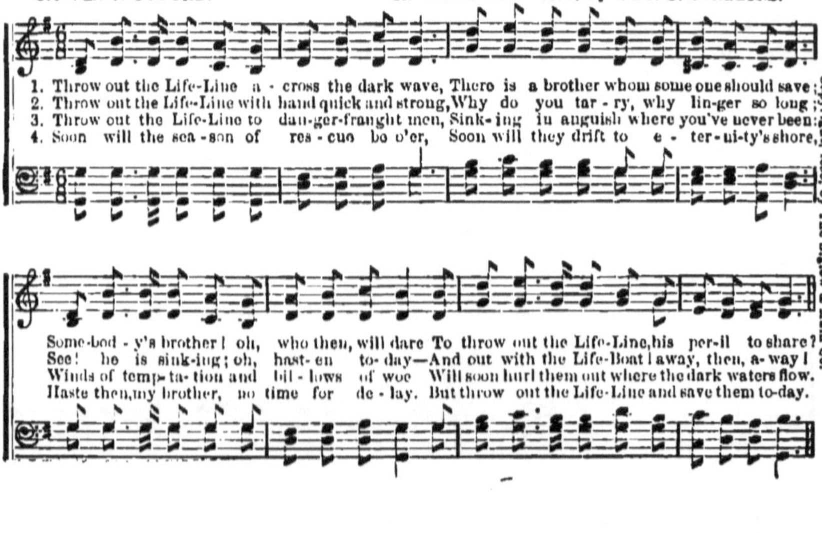

1. Throw out the Life-Line a-cross the dark wave, There is a brother whom some one should save; Some-bod-y's brother! oh, who then, will dare To throw out the Life-Line, his per-il to share?
2. Throw out the Life-Line with hand quick and strong, Why do you tar-ry, why lin-ger so long; See! he is sink-ing; oh, hast-en to-day—And out with the Life-Boat ! away, then, a-way !
3. Throw out the Life-Line to dan-ger-fraught men, Sink-ing in anguish where you've never been: Winds of temp-ta-tion and bil-lows of woe Will soon hurl them out where the dark waters flow.
4. Soon will the sea-son of res-cue be o'er, Soon will they drift to e-ter-ni-ty's shore, Haste then, my brother, no time for de-lay. But throw out the Life-Line and save them to-day.

Copyright, 1890, by The Biglow & Main Co.

Throw out the Life-Line.—Concluded.

CHORUS.

Throw out the Life-Line! Throw out the Life-Line! Some one is drift-ing a-way!

Throw out the Life-Line! Throw out the Life-Line! Some one is sink-ing to-day.

No. 148. My Mother's Prayer.

Words and Music by T. C. O'KANE.

SOLO. *Moderato.*

1. As I wandered 'round the homestead, Ma-ny a dear fa-mil-iar spot
2. Tho' the house was held by stran-gers All re-mained the same with-in;
3. Quick I drew it from the rub-bish, Cov-ered o'er with dust so long:

Brought with-in my rec-ol-lec-tion Scenes I'd seem-ing-ly for-got;
Just as when a child I ram-bled Up and down, and out and in;
When, be-hold, I heard in fan-cy Strains of one fa-mil-iar song,

There, the or-chard—mead-ow, yon-der—Here, the deep, old fash-ioned well,
To the gar-ret dark as-cend-ing—Once a source of child-ish dread—
Oft-en sung by my dear moth-er To me in that trun-dle bed;

rit.

With its old moss-cov-ered buck-et, Sent a thrill no tongue can tell.
Peer-ing thro' the mist-y cob-webs, Lo! I saw my trun-dle bed.

[*Omit*...........................

2d ending. Slow. p   *pp*

"Hush, my dear, lie still and slum-ber! Ho-ly an-gels guard thy bed!"

By per. of Ira D. Sankey, owner of Copyright.

4 While I listen to the music
   Stealing on in gentle strain,
   I am carried back to childhood—
   I am now a child again:
   'Tis the hour of my retiring,
   At the dusky eventide;
   Near my trundle bed I'm kneeling,
   As of yore, by mother's side.

5 Hands are on my head so loving,
   As they were in childhood's days;
   I, with weary tones, am trying
   To repeat the words she says:
   "Tis a prayer in language simple
   As a mother's lips can frame:
   * "Father, Thou who art in heaven,
   Hallowed, ever, be Thy name."

6 Prayer is over: to my pillow
   With a "good-night!" kiss I creep,
   Scarcely waking while I whisper,
   "Now I lay me down to sleep."
   Then my mother, o'er me bending,
   Prays in earnest words, but mild:
   * "Hear my prayer, O heavenly Fath'r,
   Bless, bless, my precious child!"

7 Yet I am but only dreaming;
   Ne'er I'll be a child again;
   Many years has that dear mother
   In the quiet churchyard lain;
   But the mem'ry of her counsels
   O'er my path a light has shed,
   Daily calling me to heaven,
   Even from my trundle bed.

* Use second ending.

No. 149. I've Found a Friend.

(Tune, No. 584, Gospel Hymns, 1-6, or G. H. Cons., No. 224. Key A.)

1 I've found a Friend; oh, such a Friend!
He loved me ere I knew Him;
He drew me with the cords of love,
And thus He bound me to Him;
And 'round my heart still closely twine
Those ties which naught can sever,
For I am His, and He is mine,
Forever and forever.

2 I've found a Friend; oh, such a Friend!
He bled, He died to save me;
And not alone the gift of life,
But His own self He gave me.
Nought that I have my own I call,
I hold it for the Giver:
My heart, my strength, my life, my all,
Are His, and His forever.

3 I've found a Friend; oh, such a Friend!
All power to Him is given;
To guard me on my onward course,
And bring me safe to heaven.
Th' eternal glories gleam afar,
To nerve my faint endeavor;
So now to watch, to work, to war,
And then to rest forever.

4 I've found a Friend; oh, such a Friend!
So kind, and true, and tender,
So wise a Counsellor and Guide,
So mighty a Defender!
From Him, who loves me now so well,
What power my soul can sever?
Shall life, or death, or earth, or hell?
No; I am His forever.

Rev. J. G. Small.

No. 149a. Jesus of Nazareth Passeth By.

(Tune, No. 9, Gospel Hymns, 1-6, or G. H. Cons., No. 8. Key G.)

1 What means this eager, anxious throng,
Which moves with busy haste along,
These wondrous gath'rings day by day?
What means this strange commotion,
In accents hushed the throng reply, [pray?
"Jesus of Nazareth passeth by."

2 Who is this Jesus? Why should He
The city move so mightily?
A passing stranger, has He skill
To move the multitude at will?
Again the stirring notes reply,
"Jesus of Nazareth passeth by."

3 Jesus! 'tis He who once below
Man's pathway trod, 'mid pain and woe;
And burdened ones, where'er He came,
Brought out their sick, and deaf and lame.
The blind rejoiced to hear the cry,
"Jesus of Nazareth passeth by."

4 Again He comes! from place to place
His holy footprints we can trace.
He pauseth at our threshold—nay,
He enters—condescends to stay.
Shall we not gladly raise the cry?
" Jesus of Nazareth passeth by."

5 Ho! all ye heavy-laden, come!
Here's pardon, comfort, rest, and home.
Ye wanderers from a Father's face,
Return, accept His proffered grace.
Ye tempted ones, there's refuge nigh,
"Jesus of Nazareth passeth by."

6 But if you still His call refuse,
And all His wondrous love abuse,
Soon will He sadly from you turn,
Your bitter prayer for pardon spurn.
"Too late! too late!" will be the cry—
"Jesus of Nazareth *has passed by.*"

Emma Campbell.

No. 150. Jesus, Saviour, Pilot Me.

Rev. EDWARD HOPPER.   (Pilot. 7s, 6 lines.)   J. E. GOULD.

1. Je - sus, Sav - iour, pi - lot me, O - ver life's tem - pest - ous sea;
2. As a moth - er stills her child, Thou canst hush the o - cean wild;
3. When at last I near the shore, And the fear - ful break - ers roar

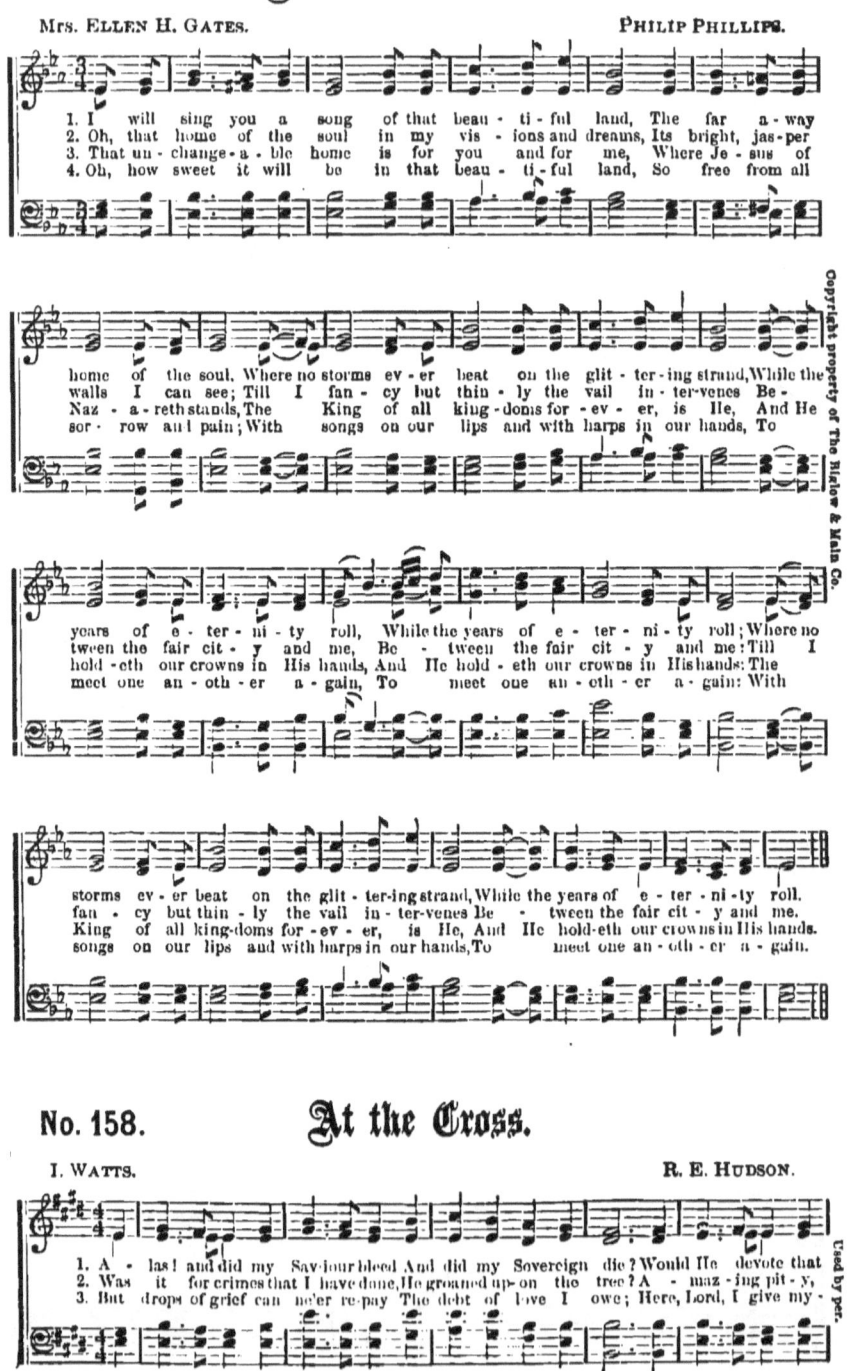

At the Cross.—Concluded.

No. 159. Jesus Shall Reign.

(Duke Street. L. M.)

ISAAC WATTS.   JOHN HATTON.

4 Blessings abound where'er He reigns
The prisoner leaps to loose his chains;
The weary find eternal rest,
And all the sons of want are blest.

5 Let every creature rise, and bring
Peculiar honors to our King;
Angels descend with songs again,
And earth repeat the loud Amen.

Abundantly Able to Save.—Concluded.

And He is a-bun - - - dant-ly a-ble to save.
And He is a-bun-dant-ly a-ble to save.

No. 163. Pray, Brethren, Pray!

Dr. HORATIUS BONAR.   PHILIP PHILLIPS.
Moderato. 

1. Pray, breth-ren, pray! The sands are fall-ing; Pray, breth-ren, pray!
2. Praise, breth-ren, praise! The skies are rend-ing; Praise, breth-ren, praise!
3. Watch, breth-ren, watch! The years are dy-ing; Watch, breth-ren, watch!
4. Look, breth-ren, look! The day is break-ing; Hark, breth-ren, hark!

Allegro.

God's voice is call-ing, You tur-ret strikes the dy-ing chime; We
The fight is end-ing, Be-hold, the glo-ry draw-eth near The
Old time is fly-ing! Watch as men watch the part-ing breath, Watch
The dead are wak-ing, With gird-ed loins all read-y stand; Be-

REFRAIN. *Slow.*

kneel up-on the verge of time:
King Him-self will soon ap-pear: } E-ter-ni-ty is draw-ing nigh!
as men watch for life or death:
hold, the Bride-groom is at hand!

ritard.   *After last verse only.*
Adagio.

E - ter - ni - ty is draw-ing nigh! is draw-ing nigh!

No. 164. Tell it Out.

FRANCES R. HAVERGAL.   Arr. by IRA D. SANKEY.

1. Tell it out a-mong the na-tions that the Lord is King; Tell it out! (Tell it out!)
2. Tell it out a-mong the peo-ple that the Sav-iour reigns; Tell it out! (Tell it out!)
3. Tell it out a-mong the peo-ple, Je-sus reigns a-bove; Tell it out! (Tell it out!)

Tell it out! (Tell it out!) Tell it out a-mong the na-tions, bid them shout and sing;
Tell it out! (Tell it out!) Tell it out a-mong the hea-then, bid them break their chains;
Tell it out! (Tell it out!) Tell it out a-mong the na-tions that His reign is love;

Tell it out! (Tell it out!) Tell it out! Tell it out with ad-o-ra-tion that He
Tell it out! (Tell it out!) Tell it out! Tell it out a-mong the weeping ones that
Tell it out! (Tell it out!) Tell it out! Tell it out a-mong the highways and the

shall in-crease, That the might-y King of glo-ry is the King of Peace; Tell it
Je-sus lives, Tell it out a-mong the wea-ry ones what rest He gives; Tell it
lanes at home, Let it ring a-cross the mountains and the o-cean's foam, That the

out with ju-bi-la-tion, let the song ne'er cease; Tell it out! (Tell it out!) Tell it out!
out a-mong the sin-ners that He came to save; Tell it out! (Tell it out!) Tell it out!
wea-ry, heav-y-la-den, need no long-er roam; Tell it out! (Tell it out!) Tell it out!

Copyright, 1894, by The Biglow & Main Co.

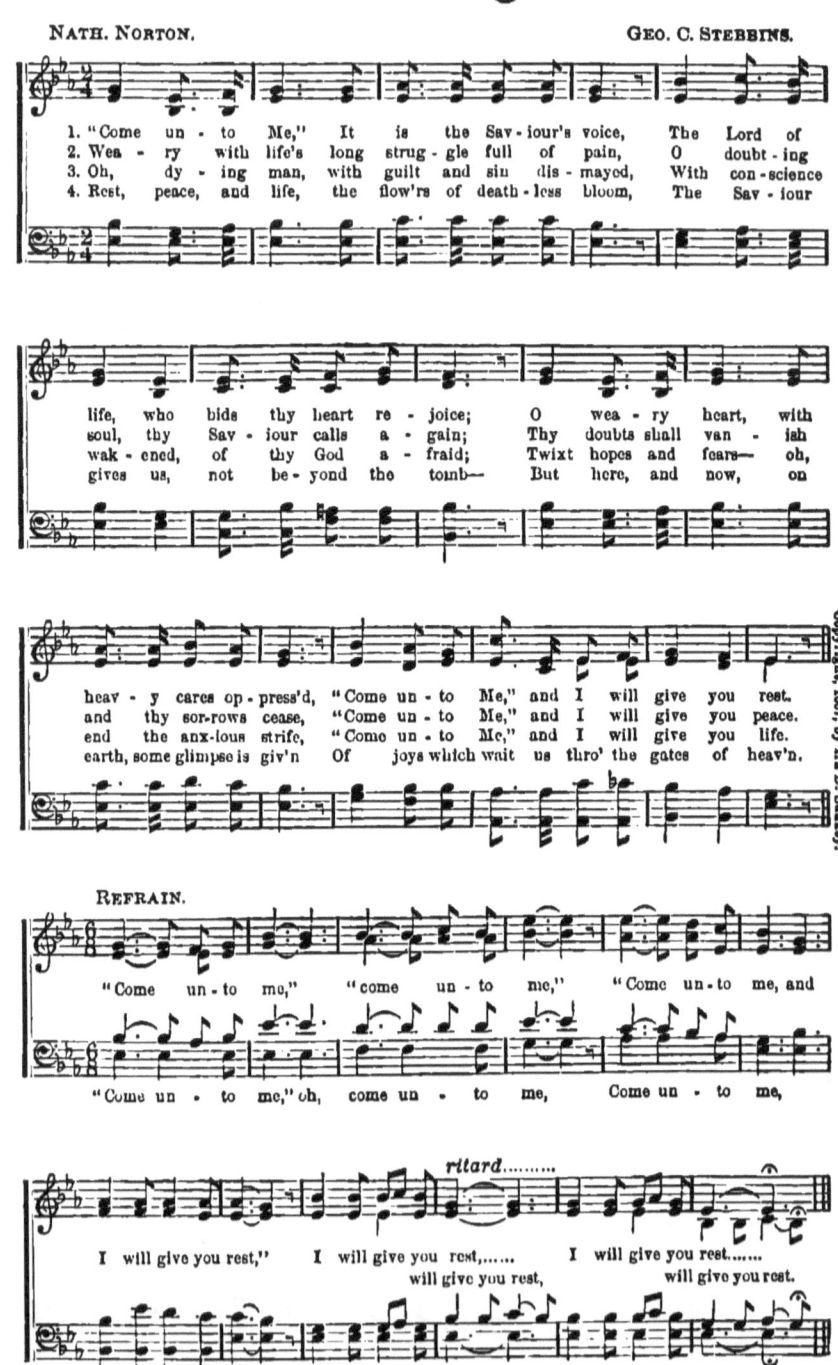

No. 168. I am Coming to the Cross.

Rev. WM. McDONALD.   WM. G. FISCHER.

4 In the promises I trust,
 Now I feel the blood applied;
 I am prostrate in the dust,
 I with Christ am crucified.

5 Jesus comes! He fills my soul!
 Perfected in Him I am;
 I am every whit made whole;
 Glory, glory to the Lamb.

No. 169. Sometime we'll Understand.

MAXWELL N. CORNELIUS, D.D.   JAMES McGRANAHAN.

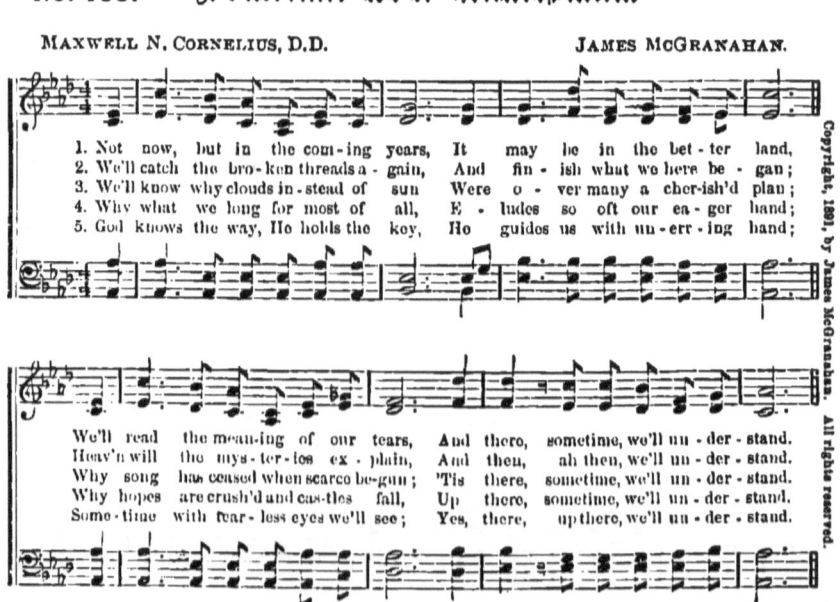

Sometime we'll Understand.—Concluded.

* Repeat for Alto only.

No. 170. I Need Thee Every Hour.

Annie S. Hawks. Robert Lowry.

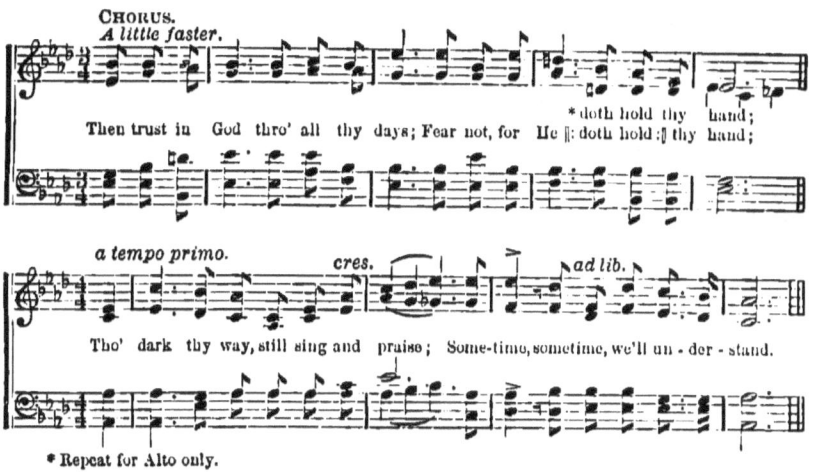

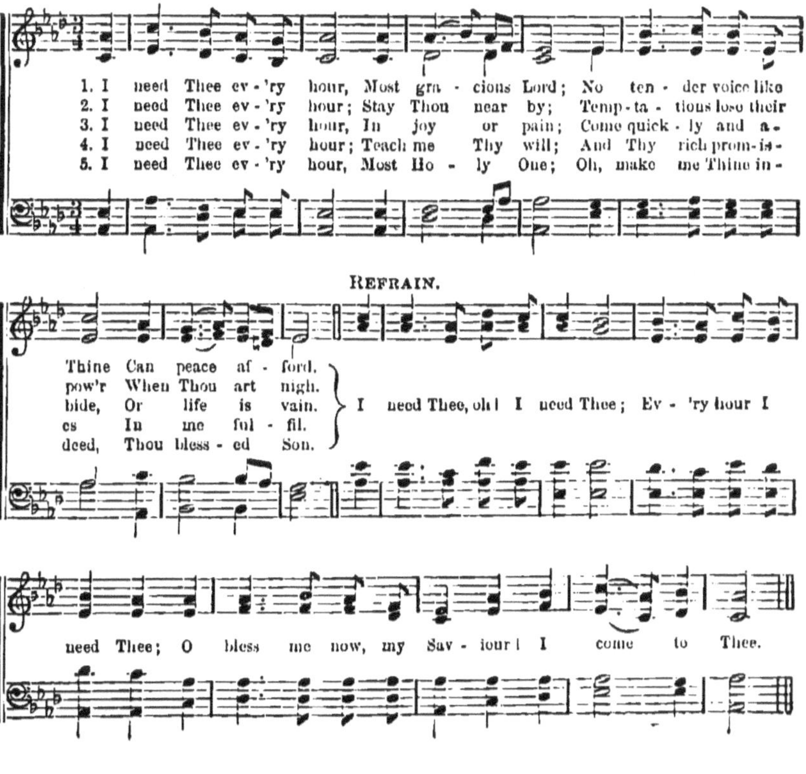

No. 171. Take Time to be Holy.

W. D. LONGSTAFF.   GEO. C. STEBBINS.

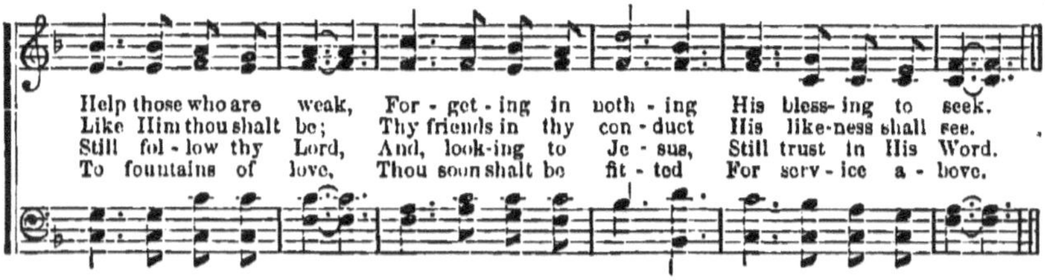

1. Take time to be ho - ly, Speak oft with thy Lord; A - bide in Him al - ways, And feed on His Word; Make friends of God's chil - dren, Help those who are weak, For - get - ing in noth - ing His bless- ing to seek.
2. Take time to be ho - ly, The world rush - es on; Spend much time in se - cret With Je - sus a - lone; By look - ing to Je - sus, Like Him thou shalt be; Thy friends in thy con - duct His like-ness shall see.
3. Take time to be ho - ly, Let Him be thy Guide, And run not be - fore Him, What - ev - er be - tide; In joy or in sor - row, Still fol - low thy Lord, And, look-ing to Je - sus, Still trust in His Word.
4. Take time to be ho - ly, Be calm in thy soul, Each thought and each mo - tive Be - neath His con - trol; Thus led by His Spir - it, To fountains of love, Thou soon shalt be fit - ted For serv - ice a - bove.

Copyright, 1890, by Ira D. Sankey.

No. 172. My Ain Countrie.

MARY LEE DEMAREST.   Mrs. I. T. HANNA. Har. by H. P. MAIN.

1. { I am far frae my hame, an' I'm wea - ry aft - en whiles, For the langed-for hame-bringin', an' my Faither's welcome smiles }
    { An' I'll ne'er be fu' con-tent, un - til my een do see The gow - den gates o' heav'n an' my *Omit* .... ain coun - trie.
D.C.—But these sights an' these soun's will as naething be to me, When I hear the an - gels singin' in my *Omit* .... ain coun - trie.

Copyright, 1881, by Biglow & Main.

My Ain Countrie.—Concluded.

{ The earth is fleck'd wi' flow-ers, mon-y-tint-ed, fresh an' gay. }
{ The bird-ies war-ble blithe-ly, for my Faith-er made them sae: }

2 I've His gude word o' promise that some gladsome day, the King
To His ain royal palace His banished hame will bring;
Wi' een an' wi' hert rinning owre, we shall see
The King in His beauty, in oor ain countrie.
My sins hae been mony, an' my sorrows hae been sair;
But there they'll never vex me, nor be remembered mair
For His bluid has made me white, an' His han' shall dry my e'e,
When He brings me hame at last, to my ain countrie.

3 Sae little noo I ken, o' yon blessed, bonnie place,
I only ken it's Hame, whaur we shall see His face;
It wad surely be eneuch for ever mair to be
In the glory o' His presence, in oor ain countrie.
Like a bairn to its mither, a wee birdie to its nest,
I wad fain be gangin' noo, unto my Saviour's breast,
For He gathers in His bosom witless, worthless lambs like me,
An' carries them Himsel', to His ain couutrie.

4 He is faithfu' that hath promised, an' He'll surely come again,
He'll keep His tryst wi' me, at what 'oor I dinna ken;
But He bids me still to wait, an' ready aye to be,
To gang at ony moment to my ain countrie.
Sae I'm watching aye, and singin' o' my hame, as I wait
For the soun'in' o' His fitfa' this side the gowden gate:
God gie His grace to ilka ane wha' listens noo to me,
That we a' may gang in gladness to oor ain countrie.

No. 173. I Heard the Voice of Jesus Say.

(Evan. C. M.)

H. BONAR, D. D.　　　　　　　　　　　　　　　WM. H. HAVERGAL.

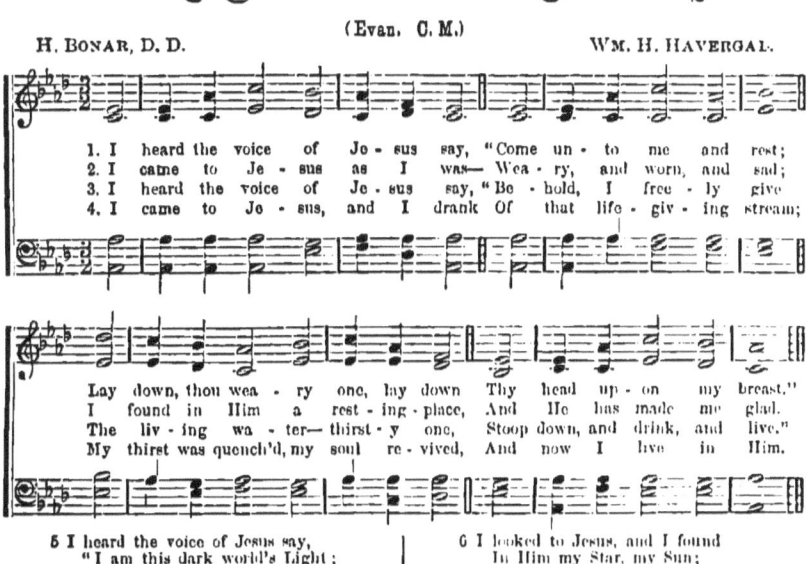

1. I heard the voice of Je-sus say, "Come un-to me and rest;
2. I came to Je-sus as I was— Wea-ry, and worn, and sad;
3. I heard the voice of Je-sus say, "Be-hold, I free-ly give
4. I came to Je-sus, and I drank Of that life-giv-ing stream;

Lay down, thou wea-ry one, lay down Thy head up-on my breast."
I found in Him a rest-ing-place, And He has made me glad.
The liv-ing wa-ter— thirst-y one, Stoop down, and drink, and live."
My thirst was quench'd, my soul re-vived, And now I live in Him.

5 I heard the voice of Jesus say,
  "I am this dark world's Light;
Look unto me, thy morn shall rise,
  And all thy day be bright."

6 I looked to Jesus, and I found
  In Him my Star, my Sun;
And in that light of life I'll walk
  'Till trav'ling days are done.

Take My Life, etc.—Concluded.

Take my hands and let them move At the im-pulse of Thy love.
Take my voice and let me sing Al-ways— on-ly— for my King.
Take my in-tel-lect, and use Ev-'ry pow'r as Thou shalt choose.
Take my heart, it is Thine own, It shall be Thy roy-al throne.
Take my-self, and I will be Ev-er, on-ly, all for Thee.

No. 176. Building for Eternity.

N. B. S.
N. B. SARGENT, arr.

Copyright, 1887, by D. B. Towner. Used by per.

1. We are build-ing in sor-row or joy, A tem-ple the world may not see,
2. Ev-'ry tho't that we've ev-er had, Its own lit-tle place has fill'd,
3. Ev-'ry word that so light-ly falls, Giv-ing some heart joy or pain,
4. Are you build-ing for God a-lone, Are you building in faith and love,

Which time can-not mar nor de-stroy, We build for e-ter-ni-ty.
Ev-'ry deed we have done good or bad, Is a stone in the tem-ple we build.
Will shine in our tem-ple walls, Or ev-er its beau-ty stain.
A tem-ple the Fa-ther will own, In the cit-y of light a-bove?

CHORUS.

We are build-ing ev-'ry day,......... A tem-ple the world may not see,
We are build-ing, build-ing, ev-'ry day,

Build-ing, build-ing ev-'ry day, Build-ing for e-ter-ni-ty.

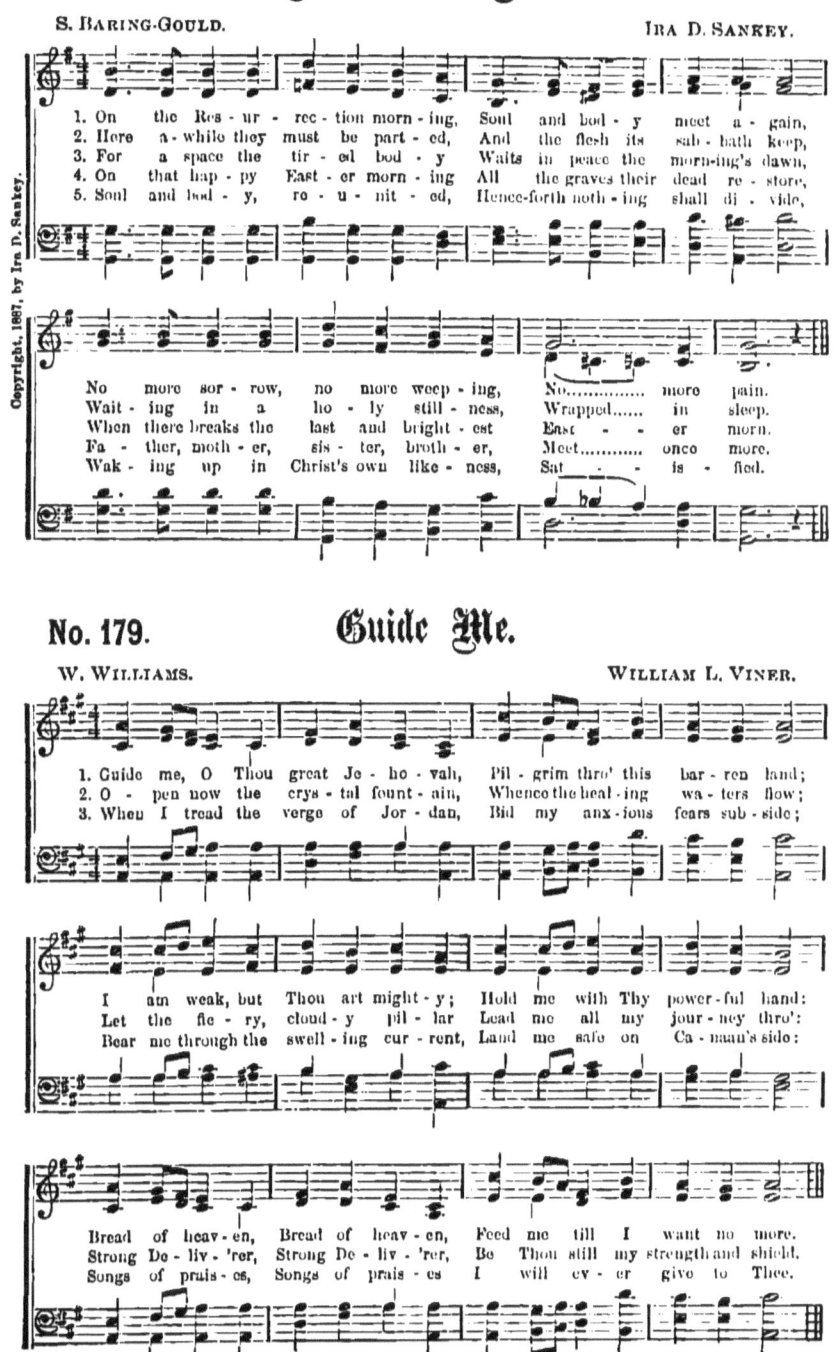

No. 180. Rescue the Perishing.

F. J. CROSBY. W. H. DOANE.

1. Rescue the perishing, Care for the dying, Snatch them in pity from sin and the grave; Weep o'er the erring one, Lift up the fallen,
2. Tho' they are slighting Him, Still He is waiting, Waiting, the penitent child to receive; Plead with them earnestly, Plead with them gently:
3. Down in the human heart, Crush'd by the tempter, Feelings lie buried that grace can restore: Touched by a loving heart, Wakened by kindness,
4. Rescue the perishing, Duty demands it; Strength for thy labor the Lord will provide: Back to the narrow way Patiently win them

CHORUS.

Tell them of Jesus the mighty to save.
He will forgive if they only believe. } Rescue the perishing,
Chords that were broken will vibrate once more.
Tell the poor wand'rer a Saviour has died.

Care for the dying; Jesus is merciful, Jesus will save.

Copyright, 1870 by W. H. Doane.

No. 181. Not all the Blood.

(Boylston. S. M.)

ISAAC WATTS. Dr. LOWELL MASON.

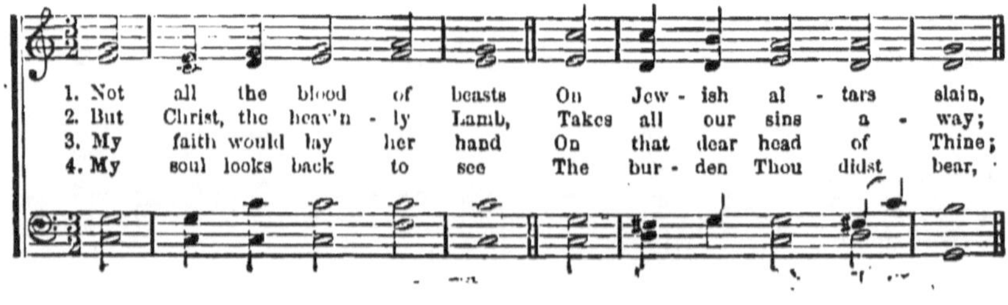

1. Not all the blood of beasts On Jewish altars slain,
2. But Christ, the heav'nly Lamb, Takes all our sins away;
3. My faith would lay her hand On that dear head of Thine;
4. My soul looks back to see The burden Thou didst bear,

Not all the Blood.—Concluded.

No. 182. Though your Sins be as Scarlet.

FANNY J. CROSBY. W. H. DOANE.

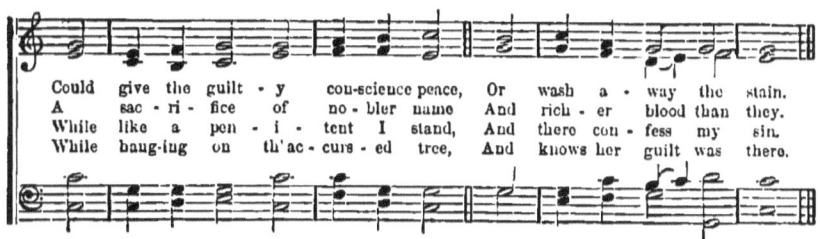

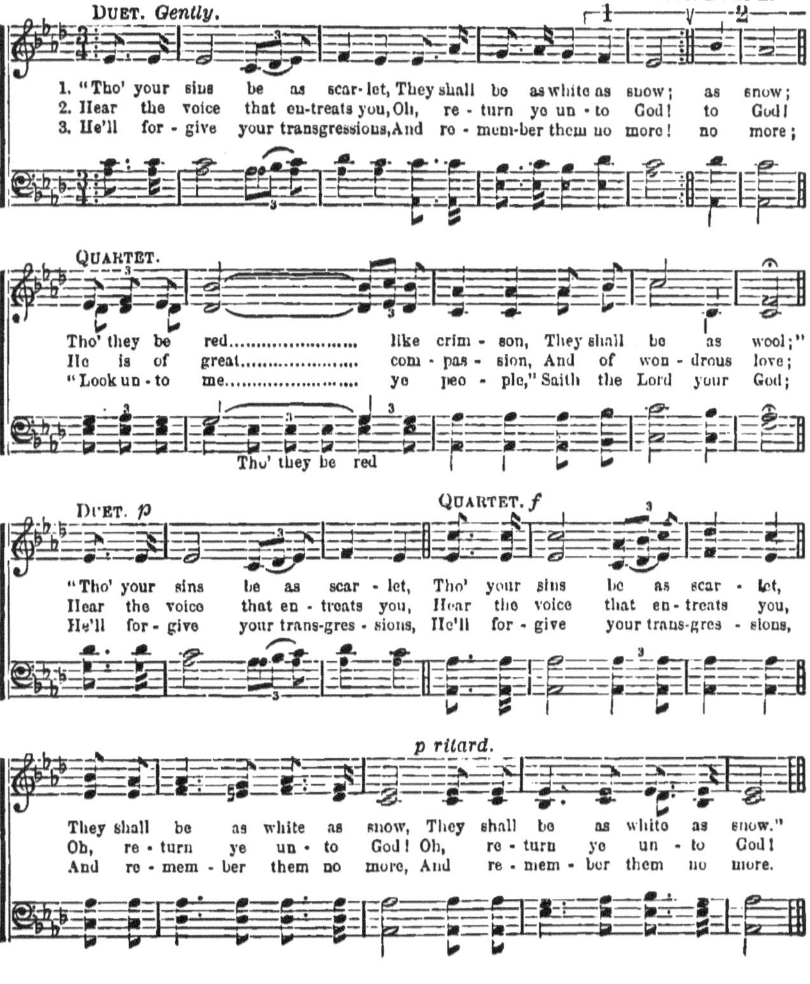

No. 183. Come, Thou Fount.
(Nettleton. 8s. 7s.)

Rev. R. ROBINSON.   JOHN WYETH.

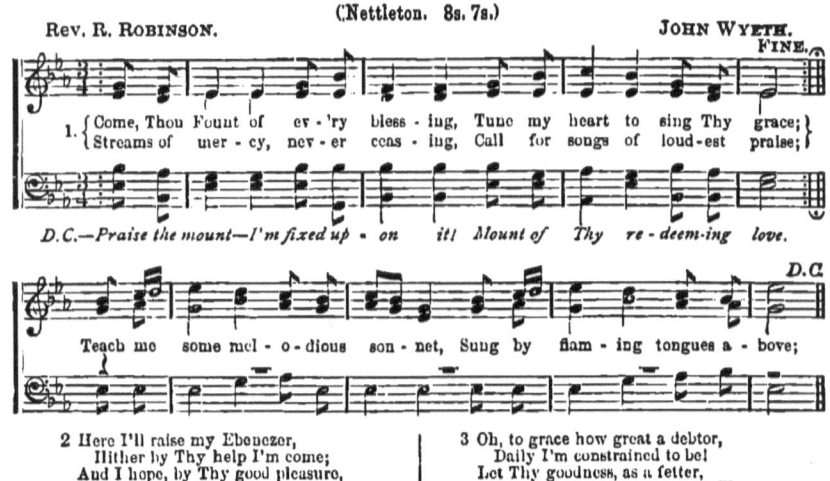

2 Here I'll raise my Ebenezer,
Hither by Thy help I'm come;
And I hope, by Thy good pleasure,
Safely to arrive at home;
Jesus sought me when a stranger,
Wandering from the fold of God;
He, to rescue me from danger,
Interposed His precious blood.

3 Oh, to grace how great a debtor,
Daily I'm constrained to be!
Let Thy goodness, as a fetter,
Bind my wandering heart to Thee;
Prone to wander, Lord, I feel it—
Prone to leave the God I love—
Here's my heart, oh, take and seal it,
Seal it for Thy courts above.

No. 184. Blest be the Tie that Binds.
(Dennis. S. M.)

Rev. JOHN FAWCETT.   H. G. NAGELI.

No. 185. Tune—Boylston. S. M. No. 181.

1 How solemn are the words,
And yet to faith how plain,
Which Jesus uttered while on earth—
"*Ye must be born again!*"

2 "*Ye must be born again!*"
For so hath God decreed;
No reformation will suffice—
'Tis *life* poor sinners need.

3 "*Ye must be born again!*"
And life *in Christ* must have;
In vain the soul may elsewhere go—
'Tis He *alone* can save.

4 "*Ye must be born again!*"
Or never enter heaven;
'Tis only blood-washed ones are there,
The ransomed and forgiven.

Anon.

No. 186. I Love Thy Kingdom, Lord.

(Shirland. S. M.)

TIMOTHY DWIGHT, D. D.   SAMUEL STANLEY.

1. I love Thy kingdom, Lord, The house of Thine abode, The Church our blest Redeemer saved With His own precious blood.
2. I love Thy Church, O God! Her walls before Thee stand, Dear as the apple of Thine eye, And graven on Thy hand.
3. For her my tears shall fall; For her my prayers ascend; To her my cares and toils be given, Till toils and cares shall end.
4. Beyond my highest joy I prize her heav'nly ways; Her sweet communion, solemn vows, Her hymns of love and praise.
5. Sure as Thy truth shall last, To Zion shall be giv'n The brightest glories earth can yield, And brighter bliss of heav'n.

No. 187. The Lord's My Shepherd.

(Belmont. C. M.)

Psalm 23.   WM. GARDINER.

1. The Lord's my Shepherd, I'll not want: He makes me down to lie In pastures green: He leadeth me The quiet waters by.
2. My soul He doth restore again; And me to walk doth make With in the paths of righteousness, E'en for His own name's sake.
3. Yea, tho' I walk in death's dark vale, Yet I will fear none ill; For Thou art with me; and Thy rod And staff me comfort still.
4. My table Thou hast furnished In presence of my foes; My head Thou dost with oil anoint, And my cup o-ver-flows.
5. Goodness and mercy all my life Shall surely follow me; And in God's house for evermore My dwelling-place shall be.

No. 188.

1 How sweet the name of Jesus sounds
   In a believer's ear;
It soothes his sorrows, heals his wounds,
   And drives away his fear.

2 It makes the wounded spirit whole,
   And calms the troubled breast;
'Tis manna to the hungry soul,
   And to the weary, rest.

3 Dear Name, the Rock on which I build,
   My shield and hiding-place;
My never-failing treasure, filled
   With boundless stores of grace.

4 Jesus my Shepherd, Saviour, Friend,
   My Prophet, Priest, and King;
My Lord, My Life, my Way, my End,-
   Accept the praise I bring.

John Newton.

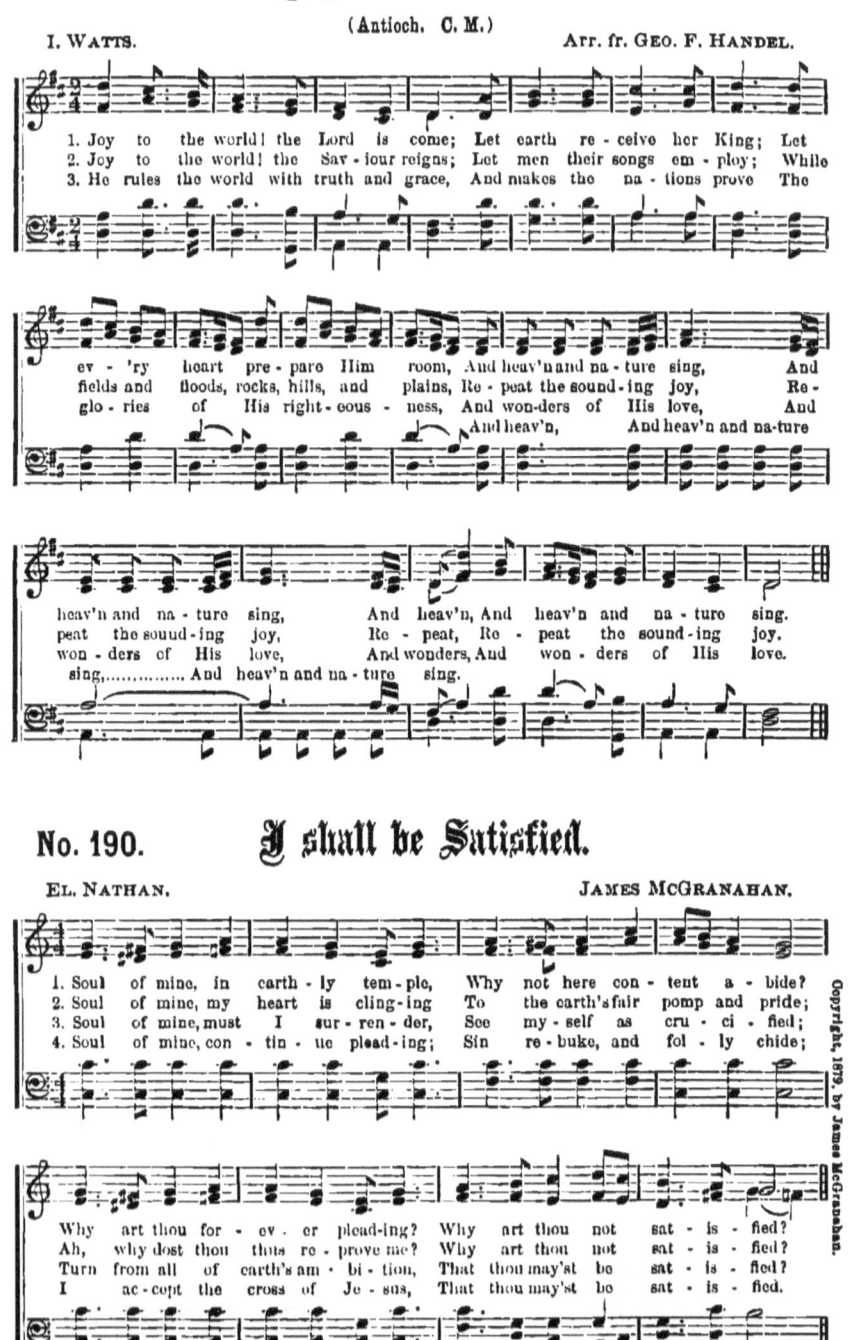

I shall be Satisfied.—Concluded.

No. 191. **Evening Prayer.**

J. EDMESTON.   GEO. C. STEBBINS.

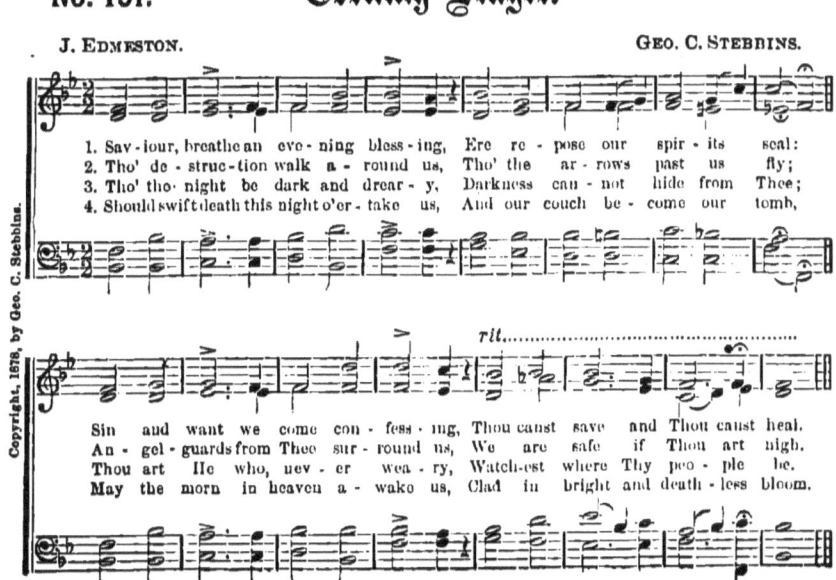

1. Sav-iour, breathe an eve-ning bless-ing, Ere re - pose our spir-its seal:
2. Tho' de - struc-tion walk a - round us, Tho' the ar - rows past us fly;
3. Tho' the night be dark and drear - y, Darkness can - not hide from Thee;
4. Should swift death this night o'er-take us, And our couch be - come our tomb,

Sin and want we come con - fess - ing, Thou canst save and Thou canst heal.
An - gel - guards from Thee sur - round us, We are safe if Thou art nigh.
Thou art He who, nev - er wea - ry, Watch-est where Thy peo - ple be.
May the morn in heaven a - wake us, Clad in bright and death - less bloom.

Copyright, 1878, by Geo. C. Stebbins.

No. 192. A Shelter in the Time of Storm.

V. J. CHARLESWORTH. IRA D. SANKEY.

1. The Lord's our Rock, in Him we hide, A shel-ter in the time of storm;
2. A shade by day, de-fence by night, A shel-ter in the time of storm;
3. The rag-ing storms may round us beat, A shel-ter in the time of storm;
4. O Rock di-vine, O Ref-uge dear, A shel-ter in the time of storm;

Se-cure what-ev-er ill be-tide, A shel-ter in the time of storm.
No fears a-larm, no foes af-fright, A shel-ter in the time of storm.
We'll nev-er leave our safe re-treat, A shel-ter in the time of storm.
Be Thou our help-er ev-er near, A shel-ter in the time of storm.

Copyright, 1885, by Ira D. Sankey.

CHORUS.

Oh, Je-sus is a Rock in a wea-ry land, A wea-ry land, a wea-ry land;

Oh, Je-sus is a Rock in a wea-ry land, A shel-ter in the time of storm.

No. 193. My Faith Looks up to Thee.

(Olivet. 6s. 4s.)

RAY PALMER, D. D. Dr. LOWELL MASON.

1. My faith looks up to Thee, Thou Lamb of Cal-va-ry, Sav-iour di-vine! Now hear me
2. May Thy rich grace im-part Strength to my fainting heart, My zeal in-spire; As thou hast
3. While life's dark maze I tread, And griefs around me spread, Be Thou my Guide; Bid darkness
4. When ends life's transient dream, When death's cold, sullen stream Shall o'er me roll, Blest Saviour!

My Faith Looks up, etc.—Concluded.

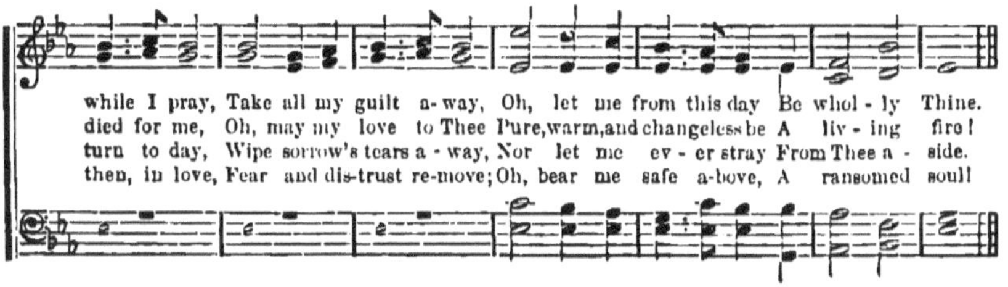

while I pray, Take all my guilt a-way, Oh, let me from this day Be whol-ly Thine.
died for me, Oh, may my love to Thee Pure, warm, and changeless be A liv-ing fire!
turn to day, Wipe sorrow's tears a-way, Nor let me ev-er stray From Thee a-side.
then, in love, Fear and dis-trust re-move; Oh, bear me safe a-bove, A ransomed soul!

No. 194. The Eye of Faith.

Rev. J. J. MAXFIELD. W. A. OGDEN.

1. I do not ask for earth-ly store Be-yond a day's sup-ply; I on-ly cov-et,
2. I care not for the emp-ty show That thoughtless worldlings see; I crave to do the
3. What-e'er the cross-es mine shall be, I will not dare to shun; I on-ly ask to
4. And when at last, my la-bor o'er, I cross the nar-row sea, Grant, Lord, that on the

more and more, The clear and sin-gle eye, To see my du-ty face to face, And
best I know, And leave the rest with Thee;—Well sat-is-fied that sweeter ward Is
live for Thee, And that Thy will be done; Thy will, O Lord, be mine each day, While
oth-er shore My soul may dwell with Thee; And learn what here I can-not know, Why

Copyright, 1891, by The Bigelow & Main Co.

CHORUS.

trust the Lord for dai-ly grace. ⎫
sure to those who trust the Lord.   ⎬ Then shall my heart keep sing-ing While to the cross I cling;
press-ing on my homeward way.   ⎪
Thou hast ev-er loved me so.   ⎭

singing, singing, cling, I cling;

For rest is sweet at Jesus' feet, While homeward faith keeps winging, While homeward faith keeps winging.

No. 195. I am Thine, O Lord.

F. J. CROSBY.   W. H. DOANE.

1. I am Thine, O Lord, I have heard Thy voice, And it told Thy love to me;
2. Con-se-crate me now to Thy ser-vice, Lord, By the pow'r of grace di-vine;
3. O the pure de-light of a sin-gle hour That be-fore Thy throne I spend,
4. There are depths of love that I can-not know Till I cross the nar-row sea,

But I long to rise in the arms of faith, And be clos-er drawn to Thee.
Let my soul look up with a stead-fast hope, And my will be lost in Thine.
When I kneel in pray'r, and with Thee my God, I com-mune as friend with friend.
There are heights of joy that I may not reach Till I rest in peace with Thee.

Copyright, 1875, by Biglow & Main.

REFRAIN.

Draw me near - er, near-er, bless-ed Lord, To the cross where Thou hast died;

near-er, near-er,

Draw me near-er, near-er, near-er, bless-ed Lord, To Thy pre-cious, bleed-ing side.

No. 196. There shall be Showers of Blessing.

EL. NATHAN.   JAMES McGRANAHAN.

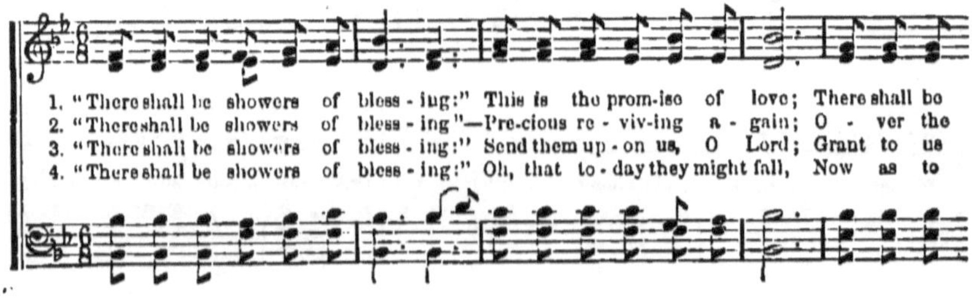

1. "There shall be showers of bless-ing:" This is the prom-ise of love; There shall be
2. "There shall be showers of bless-ing"—Pre-cious re-viv-ing a-gain; O-ver the
3. "There shall be showers of bless-ing:" Send them up-on us, O Lord; Grant to us
4. "There shall be showers of bless-ing:" Oh, that to-day they might fall, Now as to

There shall be Showers, etc.—Concluded.

CHORUS.
Show - ers of bless-ing,

sea-sons re-fresh-ing, Sent from the Sav-iour a - bove.
hills and the val - leys, Sound of a - bun-dance of rain.
now a re-fresh-ing, Come, and now hon-or Thy Word.
God we're con-fess-ing, Now as on Je-sus we call.

Showers, showers of bless-ing,

Showers of blessing we need; Mercy-drops round us are fall-ing, But for the showers we plead.

Copyright, 1883, by James McGranahan.

No. 197. Welcome! Wanderer, Welcome!

HORATIUS BONAR.   IRA D. SANKEY.

1. In the land of stran - gers, With - er thou art gone, Hear a far voice
2. "From the land of hun - ger, Faint - ing, fam-ished, lone, Come to love and
3. "Leave the haunts of ri - ot, Wast - ed, woe - be - gone, Sick at heart and

CHORUS.

call - ing, "My son! my son!"
glad - ness, "My son! my son!" } "Wel - come! wand'rer, wel - come!
wea - ry, "My son! my son!"

Welcome back to home! Thou hast wandered far a - way: Come home! come home!"

Copyright, 1884, by Ira D. Sankey.

4 "See the door still open!
  Thou art still my own;
Eyes of love are on thee,
  My son! my son!"

5 "Far off thou hast wandered;
  Wilt thou farther roam?
Come, and all is pardoned,
  My son! my son!"

6 "See the well-spread table,
  Unforgotten one!
Here is rest and plenty,
  My son! my son!"

7 "Thou art friendless, homeless,
  Hopeless, and undone;
Mine is love unchanging,
  My son! my son!"

No. 199. I Hear Thy Welcome Voice.

L. H.   Lewis Hartsough.

By per. of The Bigelow & Main Co., owners of Copyright.

1. I hear Thy wel-come voice That calls me, Lord, to Thee For cleans-ing in Thy
2. Tho' com-ing weak and vile, Thou dost my strength as-sure; Thou dost my vile-ness
3. 'Tis Je-sus calls me on To per-fect faith and love, To per-fect hope, and
4. 'Tis Je-sus who con-firms The bless-ed work with-in, By add-ing grace to

pre-cious blood That flow'd on Cal-va-ry.
ful-ly cleanse, Till spot-less all and pure.
peace,and trust, For earth and heav'n a-bove.
wel-comed grace, Where reigned the power of sin.

CHORUS.

I am com-ing Lord! Com-ing now to Thee! Wash me, cleanse me, in the blood That flow'd on Cal-va-ry.

5 And He the witness gives
To loyal hearts and free,
That every promise is fulfilled,
If faith but brings the plea.

6 All hail, atoning blood!
All hail, redeeming grace!
All hail, the Gift of Christ, our Lord,
Our Strength and Righteousness!

No. 200. In the Cross of Christ.

Sir John Bowring.   (Rathbun. 8s,7s.)   Ithamar Conkey.

Used by per. O. Ditson & Co., owners of Copyright.

1. In the cross of Christ I glo-ry, Tower-ing o'er the wrecks of time;
2. When the woes of life o'er-take me, Hopes de-ceive and fears an-noy,
3. When the sun of bliss is beam-ing Light and love up-on my way,
4. Bane and bless-ing, pain and pleas-ure, By the cross are sanc-ti-fied;

All the light of sa-cred sto-ry, Gath-ers round its head sub-lime.
Nev-er shall the cross for-sake me; Lo! it glows with peace and joy.
From the cross the ra-diance streaming, Adds new lus-ter to the day.
Peace is there, that knows no meas-ure, Joys that through all time a-bide.

No. 201. I will Pass Over You.

EL. NATHAN. JAMES McGRANAHAN.

1. When God the way of life would teach And gath-er all His own, He placed them safe beyond the
2. By Christ, the sin-less Lamb of God, The precious blood was shed, When He fulfilled God's holy
3. O soul, for thee sal-va-tion thus By God is free-ly giv'n; The blood of Christ a-tones for
4. The wrath of God that was our due, Up-on the Lamb was laid; And by the shedding of His
5. How calm the judgment hour shall pass To all who do o-bey The word of God a-bout the

Copyright, 1891, by James McGranahan. All rights reserved.

CHORUS

reach Of death, by blood a-lone.
word, And suf-fered in our stead.
sin, And makes us meet for heav'n.
blood, The debt for us was paid.
blood, And make that word their stay.

It is His word, God's precious word, It
It is His word, God's precious word,

stands for-ev-er true: When I, the Lord, shall see the blood, I will pass o-ver you.
When I, the Lord, shall see the blood,

No. 202. Christ Returneth.

H. L. TURNER. JAMES McGRANAHAN.

1. It may be at morn, when the day is a-wak-ing, When sun-light thro'
2. It may be at mid-day, it may be at twi-light, It may be, per-
3. While its hosts cry Ho-san-na, from heaven de-scend-ing, With glo-ri-fied
4. Oh, joy! oh, de-light! should we go with-out dy-ing, No sick-ness, no

Copyright, 1877, by James McGranahan, used by per.

dark-ness and shad-ow is break-ing, That Je-sus will come in the
chance, that the black-ness of mid-night Will burst in-to light in the
saints and the an-gels at-tend-ing, With grace on His brow, like a
sad-ness, no dread and no cry-ing, Caught up thro' the clouds with our

Christ Returneth.—Concluded.

No. 203. Happy Day.

P. DODDRIDGE.
From E. F. RIMBAULT.
S. CHORUS.

1. O happy day that fixed my choice On Thee, my Saviour, and my God! Well may this glowing heart rejoice, And tell its rap-tures all abroad. D.S. Happy day, happy day, When Jesus washed my sins away; He taught me how to watch and pray, And live rejoicing ev'ry day;

2. O happy bond that seals my vows
To Him who merits all my love;
Let cheerful anthems fill His house,
While to that sacred shrine I move.

3. 'Tis done, the great transaction's done;
I am my Lord's and He is mine;
He drew me, and I followed on,
Charmed to confess the voice divine.

4. Now rest, my long-divided heart,
Fixed on this blissful centre, rest;
Nor ever from thy Lord depart,
With Him of every good possessed.

5. High heaven, that heard the solemn vow,
That vow renewed shall daily hear,
Till in life's latest hour I bow,
And bless in death a bond so dear.

A Sinner like Me!—Concluded.

4 I listened: and lo! 'twas the Saviour
That was speaking so kindly to me;
I cried, " I'm the chief of sinners,
Thou canst save a poor sinner like me!"

5 I then fully trusted in Jesus;
And oh, what a joy came to me!
My heart was filled with His praises,
For saving a sinner like me.

6 No longer in darkness I'm walking,
For the light is now shining on me;
And now unto others I'm telling
How He saved a poor sinner like me.

7 And when life's journey is over,
And I the dear Saviour shall see,
I'll praise Him for ever and ever,
For saving a sinner like me.

No. 206. Nearer, My God, to Thee.

(Bethany. 6s. 4s.)

SARAH F. ADAMS. Dr. LOWELL MASON.

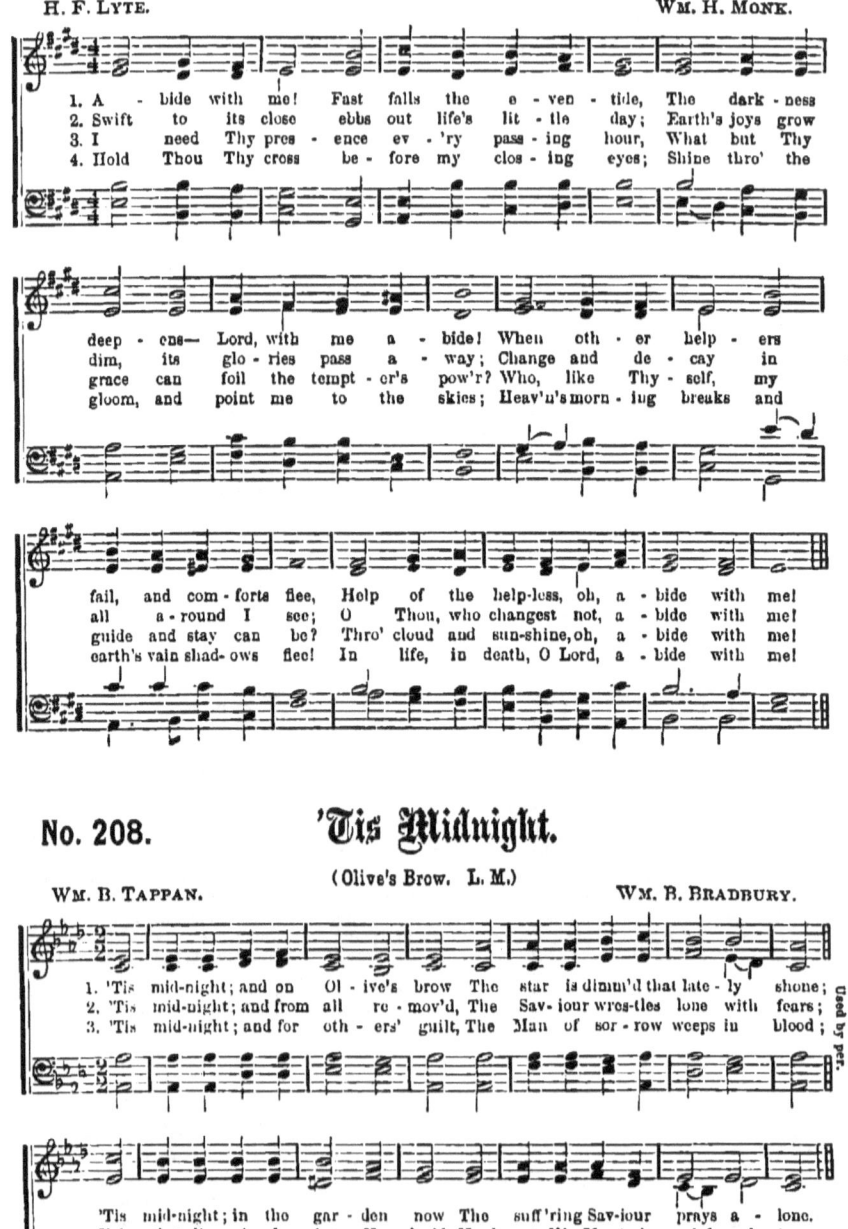

Just as I Am.—Concluded.

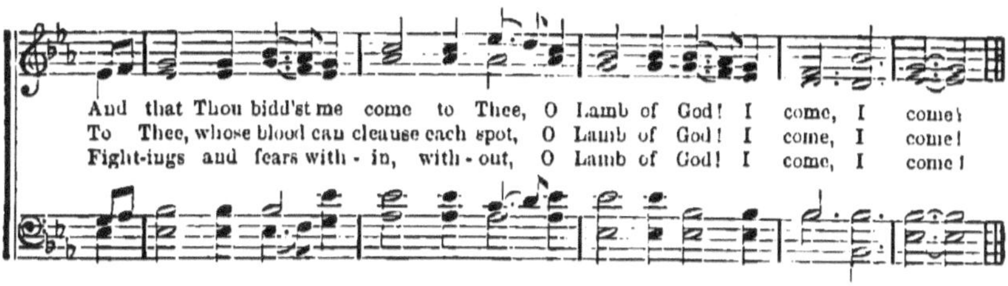

And that Thou bidd'st me come to Thee, O Lamb of God! I come, I come!
To Thee, whose blood can cleanse each spot, O Lamb of God! I come, I come!
Fightings and fears with-in, with-out, O Lamb of God! I come, I come!

4 Just as I am, poor, wretched, blind,
Sight, riches, healing of the mind,
Yea, all I need, in Thee to find,
O Lamb of God! I come, I come!

5 Just as I am; Thou wilt receive,
Wilt welcome, pardon, cleanse, relieve;
Because Thy promise I believe,
O Lamb of God! I come, I come!

No. 214. Not Now, My Child.

Mrs. PENNEFATHER.   IRA D. SANKEY.
Slow, and with expression.

1. Not now, my child,— a lit-tle more rough toss-ing, A lit-tle long-er on the bil-lows' foam; A few more journey-ings in the des-ert dark-ness, And then, the sun-shine of thy Fa-ther's Home!

2. Not now; for I have wan-d'rers in the dis-tance, And thou must call them in with pa-tient love; Not now; for I have sheep up-on the mountains, And thou must fol-low them wher-e'er they rove.

3. Not now; for I have loved ones sad and wea-ry; Wilt thou not cheer them with a kind-ly smile? Sick ones, who need thee in their lone-ly sor-row; Wilt thou not tend them yet a lit-tle while?

4 Not now; for wounded hearts are sorely bleeding,
  And thou must teach those widowed hearts to sing :
Not now; for orphans' tears are quickly falling,
  They must be gathered 'neath some sheltering wing.

5 Go, with the name of Jesus, to the dying,
  And speak that Name in all its living power ;
Why should thy fainting heart grow chill and weary?
  Canst thou not watch with Me one little hour?

6 One little hour! and then the glorious crowning,
  The golden harp-strings, and the victor's palm ;
One little hour! and then the hallelujah !
  Eternity's long, deep, thanksgiving psalm!

No. 219. **My Soul, be on Thy Guard.**

GEO. HEATH. (Laban. S. M.) Dr. LOWELL MASON.

1. My soul, be on thy guard, Ten thou-sand foes a-rise;
2. O watch, and fight, and pray; The bat-tle ne'er give o'er;
3. Ne'er think the vict-'ry won, Nor lay thine arm-or down;

The hosts of sin are press-ing hard To draw Thee from the skies,
Re-new it bold-ly ev-'ry day, And help di-vine im-plore.
The work of faith will not be done, Till thou ob-tain the crown.

No. 220. **Saviour, More than Life.**

FANNY J. CROSBY. W. H. DOANE.

1. Sav-iour, more than life to me, I am cling-ing, cling-ing close to Thee;
2. Thro' this chang-ing world be-low, Lead me gen-tly, gen-tly as I go;
3. Let me love Thee more and more, Till this fleet-ing, fleet-ing life is o'er;

Let Thy pre-cious blood ap-plied, Keep me ev-er, ev-er near Thy side.
Trust-ing Thee, I can-not stray, I can nev-er, nev-er lose my way.
Till my soul is lost in love, In a bright-er, bright-er world a-bove.

REFRAIN.

Ev-'ry day, ev-'ry hour, Let me feel Thy cleansing pow'r;

Ev-'ry day and hour, ev-'ry day and hour,

Copyright, 1875, by Biglow & Main.

Saviour, More than Life.—Concluded.

May Thy ten-der love to me Bind me clos-er, clos-er, Lord, to Thee.

No. 221. Onward, Christian Soldiers.

S. BARING-GOULD.
Presto.
A. S. SULLIVAN.

1. On-ward, Christian Sol-diers! Marching as to war, With the cross of Je-sus
2. Like a might-y ar-my Moves the Church of God: Broth-ers, we are tread-ing
3. Crowns and thrones may perish, Kingdoms rise and wane; But the Church of Je-sus
4. On-ward, then, ye faith-ful, Join our hap-py throng, Blend with ours your voi-ces,

Go-ing on be-fore, Christ, the Roy-al Mas-ter, Leads a-gainst the foe;
Where the saints have trod. We are not di-vid-ed, All one bod-y we—
Con-stant will re-main: Gates of hell can nev-er 'Gainst that Church pre-vail;
In the tri-umph song: Glo-ry, laud, and hon-or, Un-to Christ the King:

CHORUS.

For-ward in-to bat-tle, See His ban-ners go.
One in hope and doc-trine, One in char-i-ty.
We have Christ's own prom-ise— And that can-not fail.
This thro' countless a-ges Men and an-gels sing.

On-ward, Christian sol-diers!

Marching as to war, With the cross of Je-sus, Go-ing on be-fore.
With the cross of

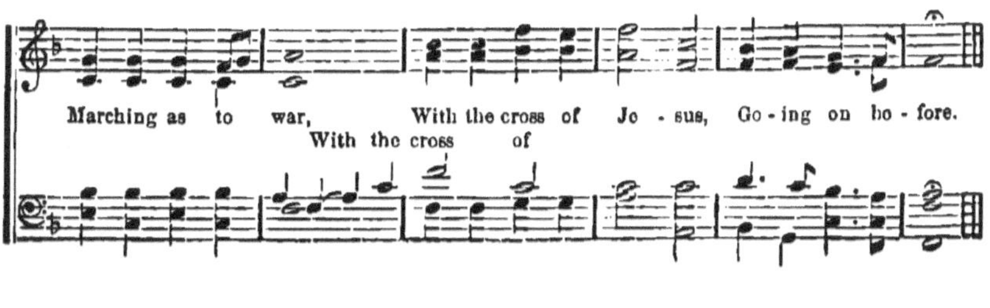

No. 225. **All Hail the Power.**

(Coronation. C. M.)

E. PERRONET. OLIVER HOLDEN.

1. All hail the power of Jesus' name! Let angels prostrate fall;
2. Let ev-'ry kindred, ev-'ry tribe, On this ter-res-trial ball,
3. Oh, that with yonder sacred throng We at His feet may fall:

Bring forth the royal diadem, And crown Him Lord of all;
To Him all majesty ascribe, And crown Him Lord of all;
We'll join the everlasting song, And crown Him Lord of all;

Bring forth the royal diadem, And crown Him Lord.......... of all.
To Him all majesty ascribe, And crown Him Lord.......... of all.
We'll join the everlasting song, And crown Him Lord.......... of all.

No. 226. **My Country 'tis of Thee.**

(America. 6s. 4s.)

S. F. SMITH, D. D. H. CAREY.

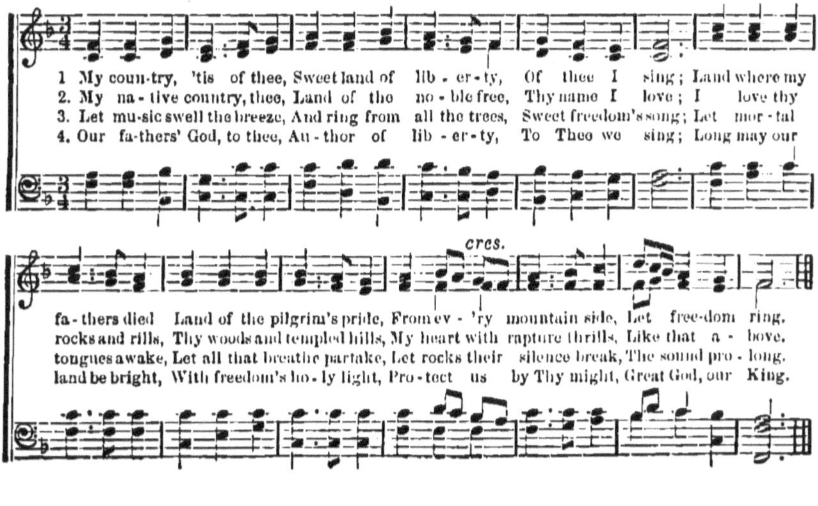

1 My country, 'tis of thee, Sweet land of liberty, Of thee I sing; Land where my
2. My native country, thee, Land of the noble free, Thy name I love; I love thy
3. Let music swell the breeze, And ring from all the trees, Sweet freedom's song; Let mortal
4. Our fathers' God, to thee, Author of liberty, To Thee we sing; Long may our

cres.

fathers died, Land of the pilgrim's pride, From ev-'ry mountain side, Let freedom ring.
rocks and rills, Thy woods and templed hills, My heart with rapture thrills, Like that above.
tongues awake, Let all that breathe partake, Let rocks their silence break, The sound prolong.
land be bright, With freedom's holy light, Protect us by Thy might, Great God, our King.

Believe and Obey.—Concluded.

bright on the way Of all who con-fess Him, be-lieve, and o-bey.

No. 232. I Steal away to Thee.

JULIA STERLING.   H. P. DANKS.

1. There is a place of ref-uge, More dear than all be-side,
2. With-in that vale of si-lence, Of calm and sweet re-pose,
3. No voice like Thine, so ten-der, Can soothe my ach-ing heart;

A vale of ho-ly si-lence, Where wea-ry souls may hide;
Where peace dis-pels all sad-ness, And like a riv-er flows;
No words like Thine, so pre-cious, Can bid my fears de-part:

And when the day is end-ed, And I from toil am free,
I hear a whis-pered mes-sage, That tells Thy love to me;
And when fall even-ing shad-ows, O wel-come hour to me!

O bless-ed, bless-ed Sav-iour, I steal a-way to Thee.
And then, by faith di-rect-ed, I steal a-way to Thee.
'Tis then for sweet com-mun-ion I steal a-way to Thee.

Copyright, 1894, by The Biglow & Main Co.

Keep Step with the Master.—Concluded.

walk............ with Christ your Sav-iour, He will lead you all the jour-ney through.
dai-ly walk

No. 234. **Bright Glory Land!**

IDA G. TREMAINE.   HUBERT P. MAIN.

1. There is a land be-yond the stars, Glo-ry Land, bright Glo-ry Land!
2. The cit-y of our God is there, Glo-ry Land, bright Glo-ry Land!
3. We lift our eyes, by faith, and see, Glo-ry Land, bright Glo-ry Land!

Be-yond the sun-set's crim-son bars,— Glo-ry Land, bright Glo-ry Land!
Its jas-per walls with beau-ty fair, Glo-ry Land, bright Glo-ry Land!
Where Christ Him-self the light shall be, Glo-ry Land, bright Glo-ry Land!

Copyright, 1894, by The Biglow & Main Co.

A land of peace with-out al-loy; Of joy be-yond all earth-ly joy;
Its gates of pearl like sil-ver gleam, Its skies with fade-less sun-light beam,
There songs of praise glad hearts shall sing; The ra-diant air with mu-sic ring;

And naught its calm can e'er de-stroy,— Glo-ry Land, bright Glo-ry Land!
And through it rolls life's crys-tal stream, Glo-ry Land, bright Glo-ry Land!
Each voice pro-claim our Sav-iour, King. Glo-ry Land, bright Glo-ry Land!

No. 236. The Christian Endeavor Army.

FANNY J. CROSBY.   IRA D. SANKEY.

1. On, march on, O Army of Endeav-'rers, On, march on with banners wide unfurled; Strike for right, the Lord Himself is with you,
2. On, march on, O Army of Endeav-'rers, On, march on, the truth shall yet prevail; Lo, in dust the foe shall fall before you,
3. Hail, all hail, O Army of Endeav-'rers, Crowd your ranks, the sword of triumph wield; He who leads will give you grace to conquer,
4. Hail, all hail, O Army of Endeav-'rers, Robe and palm are waiting you on high; Bear the cross of Christ a little longer,

CHORUS.

Shout the cry of battle o'er the world.
Trusting Him whose promise can not fail.
You shall come victorious from the field.
Tell the world the crowning day is nigh.

Storm the fort by Satan's host defended, Storm the fort, and set the pris-'ners free; Onward still, though legions rise against you, Follow Him who giveth victory.

Copyright, 1897, by The Biglow & Main Co.

Hear Me, Blessed Jesus.—Concluded.

Hap - py shall I be, Je - sus, my Re-deem - er, Look-ing un - to Thee.

No. 241. Revive Us Again.

Rev. W. P. Mackay.   John J. Husband.

1. We praise Thee, O God! for the Son of Thy love, For Je - sus who died, and is now gone a - bove.
2. We praise Thee, O God! for Thy Spir - it of light, Who has shown us our Sav - iour, and scat-tered our night.
3. All glo - ry and praise to the Lamb that was slain, Who has borne all our sins, and has cleansed ev - ery stain.
4. All glo - ry and praise to the God of all grace, Who has bought us, and sought us, and guid - ed our ways.
5. Re - vive us a - gain; fill each heart with Thy love; May each soul be re - kin - dled with fire from a - bove.

CHORUS.

Hal - le - lu - jah! Thine the glo - ry, Hal - le - lu - jah! A - men; Hal - le - lu - jah! Thine the glo - ry, Re - vive us a - gain.

No. 242. To the Rescue.

(Temperance.)   (Tune above.)

1. A foe is abroad, like a tyrant he reigns,
And his captives are groaning in fetters and chains.

Cho.—To the rescue, let us hasten; to the rescue,—away!
To the rescue of the fallen, O hasten to-day.

2. With faith in the Lord and the power of His might,
Let the armies of temp'rance their forces unite.

3. Go tell of God's love, and the demon shall fall;
Go tell them of Jesus, the Saviour of all.

4. Go seek out the lost in their bondage of sin,
There's hope for the fallen, go gather them in.

F. J. Crosby.

Copyright, 1894, by The Biglow & Main Co.

God will take Care of You.—Concluded.

ev-er you call, He will take care of you, trust Him for all.

No. 244. O Jesus, Thou art Standing.

(St. Hilda. 7s & 6s.)

W. W. How. From J. H. KNECHT.

1. O Jesus, Thou art standing Outside the fast-closed door,
2. O Jesus, Thou art knocking: And lo! that hand is scarred,
3. O Jesus, Thou art pleading In accents meek and low,—

In lowly patience waiting To pass the threshold o'er:
And thorns Thy brow encircle, And tears Thy face have marred:
"I died for you, my children, And will ye treat me so?"

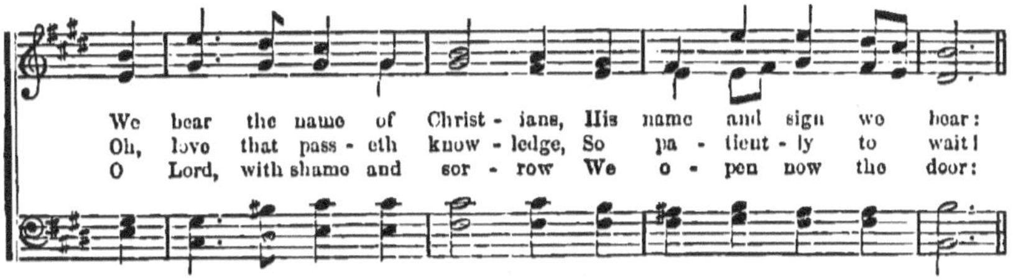

We bear the name of Christians, His name and sign we bear:
Oh, love that passeth knowledge, So patiently to wait!
O Lord, with shame and sorrow We open now the door:

Oh, shame, thrice shame upon us! To keep Him standing there.
Oh, sin that hath no equal, So fast to bar the gate!
Dear Saviour, enter, enter, And leave us nevermore!

No. 245. Holy is the Lord.

F. J. CROSBY.   WM. B. BRADBURY.

1. Ho-ly, ho-ly, ho-ly is the Lord! Sing, O ye peo-ple, glad-ly a-dore Him; Let the mount-ains trem-ble at His word, Let the hills be joy-ful be-fore Him; Might-y in wis-dom, bound-less in mer-cy, Great is Je-ho-vah, King o-ver all.

2. Praise Him, praise Him, shout a-loud for joy, Watch-man of Zi-on, her-ald the sto-ry; Sin and death His king-dom shall de-stroy, All the earth shall sing of His glo-ry; Praise Him, ye an-gels, ye who be-hold Him Robed in His splen-dor, match-less, di-vine.

3. King e-ter-nal, bless-ed be His name! So may His chil-dren glad-ly a-dore Him; When in heav'n we join the hap-py strain, When we cast our bright crowns be-fore Him; There in His like-ness joy-ful a-wak-ing, There we shall see Him, there we shall sing.

CHORUS.

Ho-ly, ho-ly, ho-ly is the Lord, Let the hills be joy-ful be-fore Him.

By per. The Biglow & Main Co., owners of Copyright.

No. 250. More about Jesus.

E. E. HEWITT. JNO. R. SWENEY.

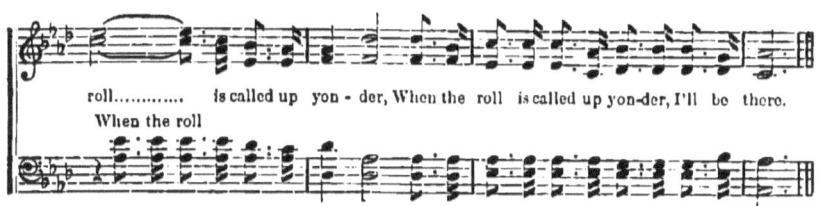

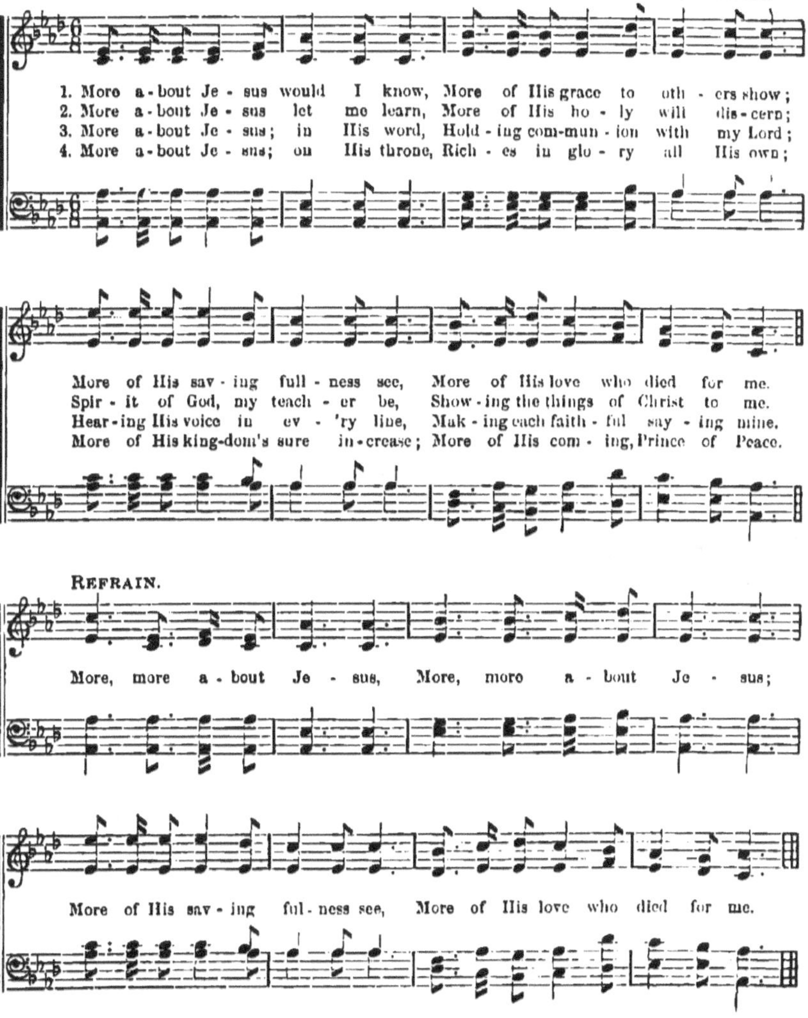

No. 251. Why Waitest Thou?

F. J. Crosby.   Ira D. Sankey.

1. Why wait-est thou, O bur-dened soul, When Je-sus now will make thee whole?
2. Why wait-est thou? why not be-lieve? His of-fered grace with joy re-ceive;
3. Why wait-est thou? the days are few, And there is work for thee to do;

Give up thy all to His con-trol, The Life, the Truth, the Way.
How canst thou still the Spir-it grieve? Thou hast no time to stay.
For-sake the wrong, the right pur-sue; A-rise! no more de-lay.

He is call-ing thee, gent-ly call-ing thee; He is call-ing thee, Gent-ly call-ing thee; O come and give Him now thy heart; He is call-ing thee to-day.

Copyright 1887, by The Biglow & Main Co.

No. 252. There's a Wideness.

Frederick W. Faber.   Lizzie S. Tourjée.

1. There's a wide-ness in God's mer-cy, Like the wide-ness of the sea;
2. There is wel-come for the sin-ner, And more grac-es for the good;
3. For the love of God is broad-er Than the meas-ure of man's mind;
4. If our love were but more sim-ple, We should take Him at His word;

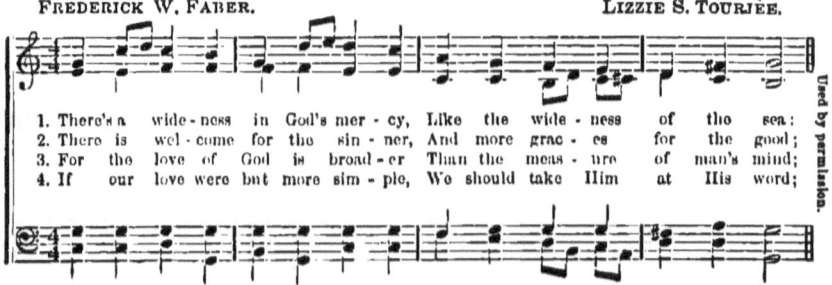

Used by permission.

There's a Wideness.—Concluded.

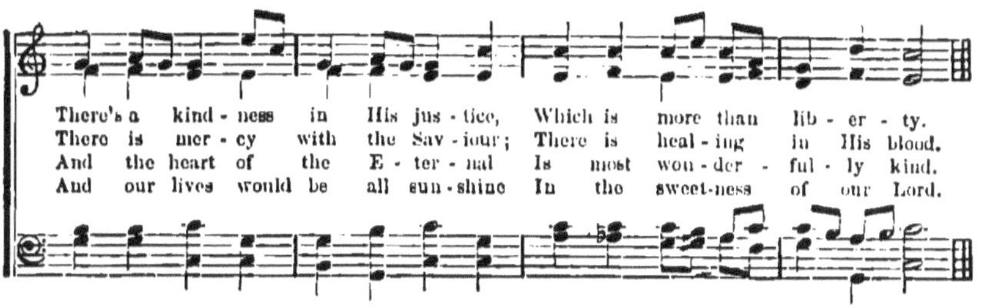

There's a kind-ness in His jus-tice, Which is more than lib-er-ty.
There is mer-cy with the Sav-iour; There is heal-ing in His blood.
And the heart of the E-ter-nal Is most won-der-ful-ly kind.
And our lives would be all sun-shine In the sweet-ness of our Lord.

No. 253. Go Bravely Forth.

CHARLES GROENENDYKE.   JAMES McGRANAHAN.

1. Go brave-ly forth to bat-tle Ye sol-diers of the Lord,
2. The Lord Him-self will lead you, Shall arm you for the fight,—
3. Leave not the path of du-ty, And none can bring you harm,
4. And, though his "name is le-gion," The foe shrinks back with shame,

Fear not, for ye shall con-quer Through His al-might-y word.
'Gainst ev-ery foe sus-tain you, And shield you by His might.
For God to shield His faith-ful, Makes bare His might-y arm.
Be-fore the fee-blest Chris-tian Who fights in Je-sus' name.

Copyright, 1897, by James McGranahan.

CHORUS.

Then brave-ly forth to bat-tle, In this, God's ho-ly strife,
And he that o-ver-com-eth, Shall gain the crown of life.

Sun of my Soul.—Concluded.

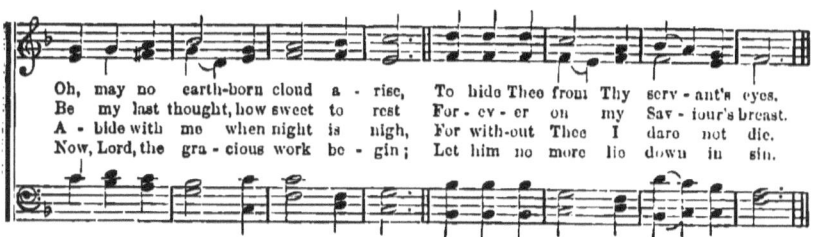

Oh, may no earth-born cloud a - rise, To hide Thee from Thy serv - ant's eyes.
Be my last thought, how sweet to rest For - ev - er on my Sav - iour's breast.
A - bide with me when night is nigh, For with-out Thee I dare not die.
Now, Lord, the gra - cious work be - gin; Let him no more lie down in sin.

No. 258. Tune.—Hursley.

1 O bless the hour when evening comes
And calls us to our place of prayer;
With joyful heart our feet we turn
To meet Thine own disciples there.

2 With one accord we gather here,
Our wants make known, our sins confess;
Dear Saviour, wilt Thou now appear
And bless, as only Thou canst bless.

3 Our faith increase, our fears remove,
Make strong the weak, the helpless raise;
May every heart now feel Thy love,
And every tongue speak forth Thy praise.

4 No want have we Thou canst not fill,
No need but Thou canst fully meet;
May we obey Thy gracious will
And find our lives in Thee complete.

Rev. N. J. SQUIRES.

No. 259. Still, still with Thee.

HARRIET B. STOWE.   IRA D. SANKEY.

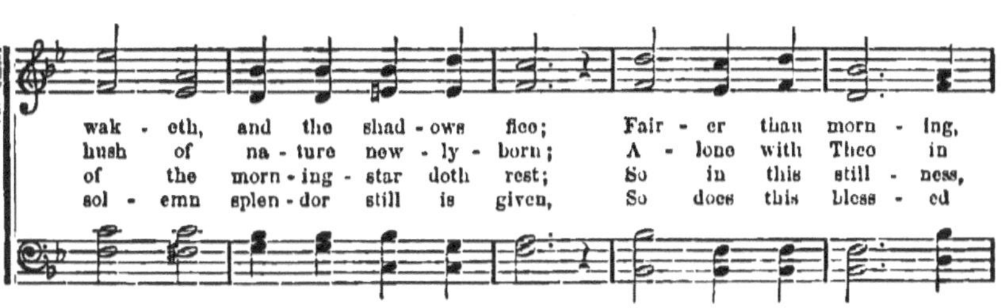

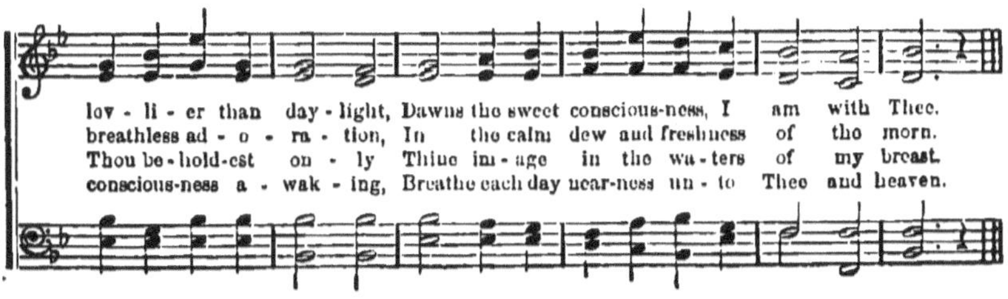

Copyright, 1884, by The Biglow & Main Co.

1. Still, still with Thee, when pur - ple morn - ing break - eth, When the bird wak - eth, and the shad - ows flee; Fair - er than morn - ing, lov - li - er than day - light, Dawns the sweet conscious-ness, I am with Thee.
2. A - lone with Thee, a - mid the mys - tic shad - ows, The sol - emn hush of na - ture new - ly - born; A - lone with Thee in breathless ad - o - ra - tion, In the calm dew and freshness of the morn.
3. As in the dawn - ing, o'er the wave - less o - cean, The im - age of the morn - ing - star doth rest; So in this still - ness, Thou be - hold - est on - ly Thine im - age in the wa - ters of my breast.
4. Still, still to Thee! as to each new - born morn - ing A fresh and sol - emn splen - dor still is given, So does this bless - ed conscious-ness a - wak - ing, Breathe each day near-ness un - to Thee and heaven.

Responsive Scripture Readings.

No. 260.　Psalm 46.

1 God is our refuge and strength, a very present help in trouble.

2 Therefore will not we fear, though the earth be removed, and though the mountains be carried into the midst of the sea;

3 Though the waters thereof roar and be troubled, though the mountains shake with the swelling thereof. Selah.

4 There is a river, the streams whereof shall make glad the city of God, the holy place of the tabernacles of the Most High.

5 God is in the midst of her; she shall not be moved: God shall help her, and that right early.

6 The heathen raged, the kingdoms were moved: he uttered his voice, the earth melted.

7 The LORD of hosts is with us; the God of Jacob is our refuge. Selah.

8 Come, behold the works of the LORD, what desolations he hath made in the earth.

9 He maketh wars to cease unto the end of the earth; he breaketh the bow, and cutteth the spear in sunder; he burneth the chariot in the fire.

10 Be still, and know that I am God: I will be exalted among the heathen, I will be exalted in the earth.

11 The LORD of hosts is with us; the God of Jacob is our refuge. Selah.

No. 261.　Psalm 121.

1 I will lift up mine eyes unto the hills, from whence cometh my help.

2 My help cometh from the LORD, which made heaven and earth.

3 He will not suffer thy foot to be moved: he that keepeth thee will not slumber.

4 Behold, he that keepeth Israel shall neither slumber nor sleep.

5 The LORD is thy keeper: the LORD is thy shade upon thy right hand.

6 The sun shall not smite thee by day, nor the moon by night.

7 The LORD shall preserve thee from all evil: he shall preserve thy soul.

8 The LORD shall preserve thy going out and thy coming in from this time forth, and even for evermore.

No. 262.　John 14: 1–14.

1 Let not your heart be troubled: ye believe in God, believe also in me.

2 In my Father's house are many mansions: if it were not so, I would have told you. I go to prepare a place for you.

3 And if I go and prepare a place for you, I will come again, and receive you unto myself; that where I am, there ye may be also.

4 And whither I go ye know, and the way ye know.

5 Thomas saith unto him, Lord, we know not whither thou goest; and how can we know the way?

6 Jesus saith unto him, I am the way, the truth, and the life: no man cometh unto the Father, but by me.

7 If ye had known me, ye should have known my Father also: and from henceforth ye know him, and have seen him.

8 Philip saith unto him, Lord, shew us the Father, and it sufficeth us.

9 Jesus saith unto him, Have I been so long time with you, and yet hast thou not known me, Philip? he that hath seen me hath seen the Father; and how sayest thou then, Shew us the Father?

10 Believest thou not that I am in the Father, and the Father in me? the words that I speak unto you I speak not of myself: but the Father that dwelleth in me, he doeth the works.

11 Believe me that I am in the Father, and the Father in me, or else believe me for the very works' sake.

Responsive Scripture Readings.

12 *Verily, verily, I say unto you, He that believeth on me, the works that I do shall he do also: and greater works than these shall he do; because I go unto my Father.*

13 And whatsoever ye shall ask in my name, that will I do, that the Father may be glorified in the Son.

14 *If ye shall ask any thing in my name, I will do it.*

No. 263. 1 Corinthians, 13.

1 Though I speak with the tongues of men and of angels, and have not charity, I am become as sounding brass, or a tinkling cymbal.

2 *And though I have the gift of prophecy, and understand all mysteries, and all knowledge; and though I have all faith, so that I could remove mountains, and have not charity, I am nothing.*

3 And though I bestow all my goods to feed the poor, and though I give my body to be burned, and have not charity, it profiteth me nothing.

4 *Charity suffereth long, and is kind; charity envieth not; charity vaunteth not itself, is not puffed up,*

5 Doth not behave itself unseemly, seeketh not her own, is not easily provoked, thinketh no evil;

6 *Rejoiceth not in iniquity, but rejoiceth in the truth;*

7 Beareth all things, believeth all things, hopeth all things, endureth all things.

8 *Charity never faileth: but whether there be prophecies, they shall fail; whether there be tongues, they shall cease; whether there be knowledge, it shall vanish away.*

9 For we know in part, and we prophesy in part.

10 *But when that which is perfect is come, then that which is in part shall be done away.*

11 When I was a child, I spake as a child, I understood as a child, I thought as a child: but when I became a man, I put away childish things.

12 *For now we see through a glass, darkly; but then face to face: now I know in part; but then shall I know even as also I am known.*

13 And now abideth faith, hope, charity, these three; but the greatest of these is charity.

No. 264. Matthew 5: (1–16.)

1 And seeing the multitudes, he went up into a mountain: and when he was set, his disciples came unto him:

2 *And he opened his mouth, and taught them, saying,*

3 Blessed are the poor in spirit: for theirs is the kingdom of heaven.

4 *Blessed are they that mourn: for they shall be comforted.*

5 Blessed are the meek: for they shall inherit the earth.

6 *Blessed are they which do hunger and thirst after righteousness: for they shall be filled.*

7 Blessed are the merciful: for they shall obtain mercy.

8 *Blessed are the pure in heart: for they shall see God.*

9 Blessed are the peacemakers: for they shall be called the children of God.

10 *Blessed are they which are persecuted for righteousness' sake: for theirs is the kingdom of heaven.*

11 Blessed are ye, when men shall revile you, and persecute you, and shall say all manner of evil against you falsely, for my sake.

12 *Rejoice, and be exceeding glad: for great is your reward in heaven: for so persecuted they the prophets which were before you.*

13 Ye are the salt of the earth: but if the salt have lost his savour, wherewith shall it be salted? it is thenceforth good for nothing, but to be cast out, and to be trodden under foot of men.

14 *Ye are the light of the world. A city that is set on a hill cannot be hid.*

15 Neither do men light a candle, and put it under a bushel, but on a candlestick; and it giveth light unto all that are in the house.

16 *Let your light so shine before men, that they may may see your good works, and glorify your Father which is in heaven.*

Motto:

"For Christ and the Church."

Active Member's Pledge

TRUSTING IN THE LORD JESUS CHRIST for strength, I promise Him that I will strive to do whatever He would like to have me do; that I will make it the rule of my life to pray and to read the Bible every day, and to support my own church in every way, especially by attending all her regular Sunday and mid-week services, unless prevented by some reason which I can conscientiously give to my Saviour; and that, just so far as I know how, throughout my whole life, I will endeavor to lead a Christian life. As an active member I promise to be true to all my duties; to be present at and to take some part, aside from singing, in every Christian Endeavor prayer-meeting, unless hindered by some reason which I can conscientiously give to my Lord and Master. If obliged to be absent from the monthly consecration-meeting of the Society, I will, if possible, send at least a verse of Scripture to be read in response to my name at the roll-call.

Benediction:

"The Lord watch between me and thee when we are absent one from another."

TOPICAL INDEX,
CHRISTIAN ENDEAVOR EDITION OF SACRED SONGS, No. 1.

ABIDING IN CHRIST.
NO.
Dying with Jesus...............102
Jesus my Lord, Thou..........103
Saviour, lead me.................204
Without Thee, my............. 50

ASSURANCE.
Blessed assurance...............161
I heard the voice.................173
My Jesus, I love..................153
My sins which were............. 4
Soul of mine, in..................190

ATONEMENT.
Christ has for sin................134
I am redeemed..................... 16
My sins which were............. 4
We come, O Lord................. 31
When God the way..............201

BIBLE.
How solemn are the............165
I will sing the....................127
When God the way..............201

BLOOD (Precious).
Alas! and did my................156
Blessed be the Fountain......130
How solemn are the............185
I am satisfied..................... 73
There is a green................125
Tho' your sins be................182
'Tis midnight! and..............208
When my life-work.............126
Who are these?...................227
Whoever receiveth..............162

CHILDREN.
Arise, young men................101
Do you fear the foe?............ 17
Hide me, O my...................151
Now I have found................ 94
Onward, onward................. 2
The Lord's our Rock...........192
Walking in the.................... 41
With the glorious................ 27

CLOSING.
Blest be the tie...................184
God be with you.................143
Praise God from..................123
When the mists..................138

COMFORT—COMFORTER.
NO.
After a long and.................. 15
After the darkest................. 80
Come, Thou Almighty........135
Go bury thy sorrow............. 43
God lives, can I................... 40
How dear to my................... 61
I've found a Friend............149
Let not your heart............... 42
Like the fullness.................. 86
Oh, spread the.................... 83

COMING OF CHRIST.
A lamp in the.....................110
Come on the wings............. 14
He is coming, the...............174
I know not when................. 90
Impatient heart................... 56
It may be at morn..............202
O Church of Christ............120
O the weary night............... 75
Some sweet morn............... 12
The night is long................. 38
There'll be no dark.............106

CONFESSION.
Am I a soldier....................137
I heard the voice................173
I need Thee every..............170
Just as I am.......................213
My Jesus I love..................153
Willing to own Thee........... 29

CONSECRATION.
All for Jesus....................... 45
I am Thine, O....................195
I come, O blessed............... 84
My life, my love.................115
Not I, but Christ................119
Saviour, more than.............220
Take my life, and...............175

CROSS AND CROWN.
Alas! and did my................156
Am I a soldier....................137
I am coming to the.............168
I am redeemed.................... 16
Nearer the Cross................212
Soul of mine in..................190
Take the jeers, and............. 25
There is a green.................125

FAITH. NO.
Encamped along.................138
I do not ask for..................194
I will sing you a................157
Jesus knows all your.......... 64
Just as I am.......................213
My faith looks up...............193

FELLOWSHIP and FOLLOWING.
Be near me, O my............. 33
Blest be the tie..................184
Guide me, O Thou..............179
If in the valley................... 58
O my Redeemer.................. 55
Take the jeers, and............. 25
Walking in the................... 41
What a fellowship..............254
When we walk with............156
Where my Saviour's hand...256

FORGIVENESS.
Alas! and did my................156
My sins which were............. 4
The dear loving Saviour......116
Tho' your sins be................182
Whosoever shall call........... 91

FRIEND (Christ a).
I've found a Friend............149
Not now, my child..............214
Now I have found............... 94
O my Redeemer.................. 55
There is no friend.............. 93
What a friend we...............140

FUNERAL.
Jesus knows all your.......... 64
No sorrow there................. 95
Not now, but in the............149
The Homeland!..................108
There'll be no dark.............106
When I shall wake..............224

GOSPEL.
Down into my..................... 34
Jesus is tenderly................132
Let us sing again................104
Sinners, Jesus will.............167
Tell the glad story..............100
Throw out the Life-...........147

GRACE.
Am I a soldier....................137
Be present at our...............117
Come, Thou Fount.............185
It doth suffice................... 28

TOPICAL INDEX, C. E. Ed. Sac. S. No. 1.—Continued.

NO.
Jesus knows all...... 64
Some day the silver............115
Whoever receiveth............162

GUIDE—GUIDANCE.
Guide me. O Thou............170
Hark! hark, my soul............160
How sweet the name............188
I lift my thankful............ 46
I was wandering and......... 49
Jesus, Saviour, Pilot............150
Lead me gently home,........247
More about Jesus............250
Saviour, lead me............204
To thee who from............210

HEAVEN.
God be with you 143
I will sing the............127
I will sing you............157
Jesus, Saviour, Pilot............150
No more the curse 96
No sorrow there............ 95
Not now, but in............169
One sweetly solemn............109
Over the river faces............211
Rejoice, Rejoice, O............ 82
Some one will enter............142
Soul of mine in............190
The Homeland!............108
There is a land............234
They tell me of a 69
We shall meet............239
When the mists have............138
When my life-work............126
When the trumpet............249

HOLY SPIRIT—HOLY GHOST.
Baptize me with the............ 52
Come, Holy Spirit............ 92
Come, Thou Almighty........135
Holy Ghost with............145
Nothing but leaves............111
Oh, spread the tidings......... 28
Spirit so holy............ 23
Take time to be holy............171
There shall be showers............196

HOPE.
Abide with Me............207
Blessed assurance............161
Some sweet morn 12

INVITATION.
"Come unto Me." It............166
Come unto Me, ye weary 63
God is now willing............ 77
I heard the voice............173
I hear Thy welcome............199
In the land of............197

NO.
Jesus is tenderly............132
Jesus knocks; He calls......... 9
Just as I am............213
Look unto me............ 35
O how can you live............ 89
O tender and sweet............217
Resting my soul............ 11
The Master is come............ 18
Throw out the Life-............147
To Thee who from............210
Where is my wand'ring........255
Why waitest thou............251
Would you be forever.......... 76

JOY.
Awake, awake, O heart of......124
Come, Thou Fount............183
Do you fear the............ 17
Hark! hark my............160
I will bless the............ 65
I will sing the............127
Joy to the world............189
Let us sing again............104
O happy day that............203
O how happy are............ 89
O sing of my............ 83
O wanderer rejoice............ 43
Rejoice! the Lord............ 10
There's sunshine in............ 44
The trusting heart............ 73
Walking in the sunshine...... 61

LIFE AND LIGHT.
"Come unto Me." It............166
How solemn are the............185
Life is mine 68
Not I, but Christ............119
O pilgrims thro' a............ 32
The Day-Star hath............ 81

LOVE.
After the darkest............ 80
God is love, His............ 99
Jesus, Lover of my............177
Like the fullness............ 86
More love to Thee............146
My Jesus I love............153
O Lord, my Soul............246
Rescue the perishing............180
There comes to my............121
There's a wideness............252
What a blessed hope............ 98

LOYALTY AND OBEDIENCE.
Arise, young men............101
For Christ and the............235
Let us stand up for 8
One sweetly solemn............109
True-hearted............131
Upon the western............112
Where my Redeemer........... 13

MISCELLANEOUS.
NO.
As I wandered round............146
I am far frae my 172
My country! 'tis of............226
Thro' the shining............114
Trembling soul, beset............107

MISSIONARY.
Jesus shall reign............159
O Church of Christ............120
Speed away............136
Tell it out among............164
Tell the glad story............100
There's a call comes............229
There's a royal............230
Ye Christian heralds............ 72

PEACE.
Abide with Me............207
"Come unto Me." It............166
Dying with Jesus............102
I am coming to............168
I heard the voice............173
Jesus knows all 64
Resting my soul 11
There comes to my............121
When I shall wake............224

PRAISE.
All hail the power............222-225
Holy! Holy! Holy!............141
I am redeemed............ 16
I do not ask for............194
I will sing the............127
O happy day that............203
Praise God from whom........123
Praise to the Holy............ 1
We praise Thee............241
When the sinner turns......... 6

PRAYER.
Be near me, O 33
Come, Thou Fount............183
Hear me, blessed............240
Hear us, O Saviour............133
Nearer, my God............206
Night had fallen............ 87
O bless the hour............258
O my Redeemer............ 55
Pass me not............154
Pray, brethren, pray............183
Saviour, breathe an............191
Sweet hour of prayer............139
There shall be showers............196
What a friend we............140

PROMISES.
How firm a foundation........152
I heard the voice............173
There shall be............196
Whoever receiveth the........162

RACE (The Christian).
Arise, young men............101
Onward, onward looking...... 2
The weary shadows............ 51
We come, O Lord............ 31

TOPICAL INDEX, C. E. ED. SAC. S. No. 1.—*Continued.* 235

REDEMPTION.
	NO.
Blessed be the fountain	130
Christ hath redeem-	60
How solemn are	185
I am coming to	168
I am redeemed	16
I was once far	205
Jesus is tenderly	132
Jesus, my Lord, to	215
Life is mine	68
Look unto me	35
My sins which were	4
O Jesus, Thou art	244
Rescue the perishing	180
Sinners, Jesus will	167
Some day the silver	118
Some one will enter	142
The dear loving Saviour	116
Tho' your sins be	182
When God the way	201
Whoever receiveth the	162
Whosoever shall call	91

REFUGE—ROCK.
Build ye on the	36
How firm a found-	152
Jesus, Lover of my	177
Rock of Ages	216
Thou art my Rock	71
Thou art, O Lord, my	37

REPENTANCE.
Alas! and did my	158
Down into my	34
I come, O blessed	84
I've wandered far	67
Jesus, my Lord, to	215
My sins which were	4
My soul is sad	62
O Jesus, Thou art	244
O wanderer, on a	10
Sinners, Jesus will	167

REST.
"Come unto Me." It	166
Dying with Jesus	102
I heard the voice	173
Life is mine	68
Resting my soul	11

RESURRECTION.
Christ has risen	39
Low in the grave	165
On the Resurrection	178
See the place where	24
Some sweet morn	12
There'll be no dark	106

SAFETY—SECURITY.
Abide with Me	207
Anywhere with Jesus	237
Come, Thou Fount	183
Dying with Jesus	102

	NO.
God will take care	243
He lives and loves	129
Hide me, O my	161
I am satisfied with	73
Keep Thou my way	47
O happy day that	203
Saviour, breathe an	191
Soul of mine in	190
Still, still with	259
The Lord's my Rock	192
There is a place of	232
Under His wings	5
We are building in	176
Ye shall know	57

SAVIOUR—SEEKING.
A wondrous boon	97
Christ alone is	21
Christ has for sin	134
I am coming to the	168
Jesus is tenderly	132
Jesus only, 'mid the	7
Jesus, Saviour, Pilot	150
Look unto me	35
O wanderer, dost	22
Rescue the perishing	180
Sinners, Jesus will	167
Throw out the Life-	147
Whoever receiveth the	162

SHEPHERD.
He feedeth His flock	79
I was wandering sad and	49
Saviour, lead me	204
The Lord's my Shepherd	187
There were ninety and	198

TEMPERANCE.
A foe is abroad	242
Down into my	34
I've found a friend	149
Rescue the perishing	180
Take courage, temperance	155
Where is my wand-	255

TRUST.
Hear us, O Saviour	133
He lives and loves	129
I am coming to	168
Jesus knows all your	64
Look unto me	35
My Jesus, as Thou	144
Not now, but in the	169
Press onward, press	231
Saviour, more than	220
Soul of mine in	190
There is never a day	122
The trusting heart	78
Trembling soul, beset	107
When we walk with	156
When the thick clouds	20

VICTORY.
	NO.
Arise, young men	101
Encamped along the	128
Enthroned is Jesus	235
Onward, Christian soldiers	221
True-hearted! whole-	131
We're soldiers of	30

WARFARE.
Am I a soldier	137
Arise, young men	101
Christian soldiers all	228
Down with the evil	74
Encamped along the	128
Go bravely forth to	253
Keep step with the	233
Let us stand up	8
My soul, be on thy	219
Move forward, valiant	223
On, march on, O	236
Onward, Christian soldiers	221
There's a royal	230
True-hearted! whole-	131
We're soldiers of	30
When the trumpet	249
Who is on the Lord's	248

WORK—WORKS.
Going forth at	113
Go work to-day	3
Lift up your eyes	85
Rescue the perishing	180
Sowing in the	209
We are building	176
With the glorious	27

WORSHIP.
All hail the power	222, 225
As I wandered 'round	148
Blessed Saviour, hear	26, 54
Come, Thou Almighty	135
Glory be to the	218
Guide me, O Thou	179
Hear us, O Saviour	133
Holy! holy! holy! Lord	141
Holy is the Lord	245
How firm a found-	152
How sweet the name	188
I love Thy kingdom	186
I need Thee every	170
I will sing the	127
I will sing you	157
Jesus shall reign	159
Let not thy heart	105
Nearer, my God, to	206
O sing that song	66
Saviour, breathe an	191
Sun of my soul	257
Sweet hour of prayer	139
Thou, whose hand	70

INDEX.

TITLES IN SMALL CAPS—FIRST LINES IN ROMAN.

	No.		No.
A foe is abroad, like a tyrant he	242	BRIGHT GLORY LAND!	234
A lamp in the night, a song in	110	BRINGING IN THE SHEAVES	209
A SHELTER IN THE TIME OF STORM	192	BUILDING FOR ETERNITY	176
A SINNER LIKE ME	205	BUILD YE ON THE ROCK	36
A SOLDIER OF THE CROSS	137		
A wond'rous boon to man is given	97	CHRIST AND THE CHURCH	235
ABIDE WITH ME	207	CHRIST ALONE IS SAVIOUR	21
ABIDE WITH ME EVER	50	CHRIST AROSE	165
Abide with me fast flows	207	Christ has for us atonement made	134
ABUNDANTLY ABLE TO SAVE	162	CHRIST HAS RISEN	39
After a long and weary strife	15	CHRIST HATH REDEEMED US	60
AFTER THE DARKEST HOUR	80	CHRIST RECEIVETH SINFUL MEN	167
Alas! and did my Saviour bleed	158	CHRIST RETURNETH	202
ALL HAIL THE POWER	225	Christian soldiers all, hear our	228
All hail the power of Jesus'	222	COME, HOLY SPIRIT, COME	92
ALL FOR JESUS	45	COME HOME	10
AMERICA. 6s, 4s	226	COME ON THE WINGS OF THE	14
Am I a soldier of the cross	137	COME THOU ALMIGHTY KING	135
ANTIOCH. C. M.	189	COME, THOU FOUNT	183
ANYWHERE WITH JESUS	237	COME UNTO ME	166
ARE YOU A REAPER?	85	COME UNTO ME, YE WEARY	63
ARISE, YOUNG MEN, ARISE	101	COMFORTED	15
As I wandered 'round the	148	COMFORT YE ONE ANOTHER	42
AT THAT DAY YE SHALL KNOW	57	CORONATION. C. M.	225
AT THE CROSS	158	COUNTED WORTHY	25
AWAKE, AWAKE! O HEART	124	CREATE IN ME A CLEAN HEART	62
		DENNIS. S. M.	184
BAPTIZE ME WITH THE SPIRIT	52	Do you fear the foe will in the	17
BE NEAR ME, O MY SAVIOUR	33	Down into my loneliness, sorrow	34
Be present at our table, Lord	117	Down with the evil and up	74
BELIEVE AND OBEY	231	Dying with Jesus, by death	102
BELMONT. C. M.	187	DUKE STREET. L. M.	159
BETHANY. 6s, 4s	206		
BLESSED ASSURANCE	161	Encamped along the hills of	128
BLESSED BE THE FOUNTAIN	130	ENDEAVORERS' MARCHING SONG	228
BLESSED SAVIOUR, HEAR MY	26	ENTHRONED IS JESUS NOW	238
Blessed Saviour, hear Thou me	54	EVAN. C. M.	173
BLEST BE THE TIE THAT BINDS	184	EVENING PRAYER	191
BOYLSTON. S. M.	181	EYE HATH NOT SEEN	69

	No.		No.
Faith is the Victory	128	I am Coming to the Cross	168
For Christ and the Church	235	I am far frae my hame	172
Gather in the Sheaves	27	I am Redeemed	16
Gerar. S. M.	92	I am Satisfied with Jesus	73
Give Me Thy Heart	210	I am the Light	32
Give Your Heart to Jesus	76	I am Thine, O Lord	195
Glory be to the Father, and to	218	I Come, O Blessed Lord	84
Gloria Patri	218	I do not ask for earthly store	194
Go bury thy sorrow	43	I Heard the Voice of Jesus Say	173
Go bravely forth	253	I Hear Thy Welcome Voice	199
Go Tell it to Jesus	43	I know not when the Lord will	90
Go Work To-day	3	I lift my thankful song	46
God Be With You	143	I Love Thy Kingdom, Lord	186
God Heareth Prayer	105	I Need Thee Every Hour	170
God is Love	99	I Shall be Satisfied	190
God is Now Willing; are You?	77	I Steal Away to Thee	232
God is now willing in Christ	77	I was once far away from the	205
God Lives	40	I was wandering, sad and weary	49
God Will Take Care of You	243	I will Bless the Lord	65
God's Bounty	86	I will Pass Over You	201
Going forth at Christ's command	113	I will Sing the Wond'rous	127
Grace Before and After Meat	117	I will sing you a song	157
Guide Me. 8s, 7s	179	I will Trust, and Not be Afraid	20
		If in the valley where the bright	58
Happy Day	203	I'll Live for Thee	115
Hark! Hark! My Soul	160	Immanuel, Prince of Peace	66
Hear Me, Blessed Jesus	240	Impatient Heart, be Still	56
Hear Thou Me	54	In the Cross	200
Hear Us, O Saviour	133	In the land of strangers	197
He Feedeth His Flock	79	Italian Hymn. 6s, 4s	135
He is Coming	174	It doth suffice, that precious	28
He is Near	90	It may be at morn when the	202
He lives and loves, our Saviour	129	I've Found a Friend	149
He Saves Me	116	I've wandered far away from	67
He Shall Reign from Sea to Sea	120		
Hide Me	151	Jesus has Taken Them All	4
Holy Ghost, with Light Divine	145	Jesus is Calling	132
Holy! Holy! Lord God Almighty	141	Jesus is Mine	94
Holy is the Lord	245	Jesus is tenderly calling thee	132
Home of the Soul	157	Jesus knocks; He calls to thee	9
How Can You Live Without	89	Jesus knows all, all your sorrow	64
How Dear to My Heart	61	Jesus Knows Your Sorrow	64
How Firm a Foundation	152	Jesus, Lover of my Soul	177
How Long	51	Jesus, my Lord, thou art my	103
How solemn are the words	185	Jesus, my Lord, to Thee I cry	215
How sweet the name of Jesus	188	Jesus of Nazareth	149a
How They Sing Up Yonder	6	Jesus Only, Jesus Ever	7
Hursley. L. M.	257	Jesus only, mid the turmoil	7

Jesus Saviour, Pilot Me	150
Jesus Shall Reign	159
Joy to the World	189
Just as I am	213
Keep Step with the Master	233
Keep Thou my Way	47
Laban. S. M.	219
Lead Me Gently Home, Father	247
Lead Me Saviour	204
Let not thy heart despair	105
Let not your heart be troubled	42
Let the Sunshine In	17
Let Us Crown Him	222
Let Us Sing Again	104
Let Us Stand for Jesus	8
Let us stand up for Jesus	8
Life is Mine	68
Lift up your eyes to the fields	85
Like the fulness of the ocean	86
Look Unto Me	35
Looking this Way	211
Lord, I'm Coming Home	67
Lord, Teach Us How to Pray	53
Low in the grave he lay	165
Loyalty to Christ	112
Make Me Willing	29
Martyn. 7s D.	177
Mercy. 7s	145
Missionary Chant. L. M.	72
Moment by Moment	102
More About Jesus	250
More Love to Thee, O Christ	146
Morning Breaks Upon	24
Move Forward	223
My Ain Countrie	172
My Country, 'Tis of Thee	226
My Faith Looks Up to Thee	193
My Grace is Sufficient	28
My Hiding Place	37
My Jesus, as Thou Wilt	144
My Jesus, I Love Thee	153
My life, my love, I give to Thee	115
My Mother's Prayer	148
My Saviour First of All	126
My sins which were many in	4
My Soul be on Thy Guard	219
My soul is sad and sinful	62
Near to Thee	70
Nearer, My God, to Thee	206
Nearer the Cross	212
Nettleton. 8s, 7s	183
Night had fallen on the city	87
No Friend Like Jesus	93
No More	96
No Sorrow There	95
Not All the Blood of Beasts	181
Nothing but Leaves	111
Not I, But Christ	119
Not now, but in the coming	169
Not Now, My Child	214
Now I have found a Friend	94
O bless the hour when evening	258
O Church of Christ! behold at	120
O happy day that fixed my choice	203
O how can you live without	89
O How Happy are They	59
O Jesus, Thou art Standing	244
O Lord, my soul rejoiceth in Thee	246
O my Redeemer	55
O pilgrims through a desert	32
O Sing of My Redeemer	83
O the weary night is waning	75
O wanderer, dost thou hear	22
O wanderer on a dreary waste	10
O Wanderer, Rejoice	48
Oh, sing that song to me again	66
Oh, spread the tidings round	88
Oh, tender and sweet was the	217
Old Hundred. L. M.	123
Olive's Brow. L. M.	208
Olivet. 6s, 4s.	193
One Sweetly Solemn Thought	109
On, march on, O Army of	236
On the resurrection morning	178
Onward, Christian Soldiers	221
Onward, Onward!	2
Open Wide the Door	9
Our Names in Heaven	82
Our Saviour King	129
Ours is the Victory	74
Over the Line	217

	No.		No.
Over the river, faces I see	211	SUN OF MY SOUL	257
		SUNSHINE IN THE SOUL	44
PASS ME NOT	154	SWEET HOUR OF PRAYER	139
PAUL AND SILAS	87	SWEET PEACE, THE GIFT OF GOD'S	121
PILOT. 7s, 6 lines	150		
PLEASURES FOREVERMORE	46	Take courage, temperance workers	155
PORTUGUESE HYMN. 11s	152	TAKE ME AS I AM	215
PRAISE GOD FROM WHOM	123	TAKE MY LIFE	175
PRAISE TO THE HOLY ONE	1	Take the jeers and take the	25
PRAY, BRETHREN, PRAY	163	TAKE TIME TO BE HOLY	171
Press onward, press onward	231	TELL IT AGAIN	100
		TELL IT OUT	164
		Tell the glad story of Jesus	100
RATHBUN. 8s, 7s	200	THE BANNER OF THE CROSS	230
REFUGE. 7s D.	177	THE DAY-STAR HATH RISEN	81
Rejoice, rejoice, O child of light	82	The dear, loving Saviour has	116
REJOICE! THE LORD IS KING	19	THE COMFORTER HAS COME	88
RESCUE THE PERISHING	180	THE CHRISTIAN ENDEAVOR ARMY	236
Resting my soul on Jesus	11	THE EVERLASTING ARMS	254
RESTING ON JESUS	11	THE EYE OF FAITH	194
RESURRECTION MORN	178	THE HOMELAND	108
REVIVE US AGAIN	241	THE HOPE OF THE COMING	110
ROCKINGHAM. L. M.	117	THE LORD'S MY SHEPHERD	187
ROCK OF AGES	216	The Lord's our Rock; in Him	192
		THE LOVE OF JESUS	98
SATISFIED	224	THE MAN OF GALILEE	97
SAVED BY GRACE	118	THE MASTER IS CALLING	18
SAVED TO-NIGHT	34	The Master is come, and is	18
SAVED TO SERVE	113	The night is long and dreary	38
Saviour, breathe an evening	191	THE NINETY AND NINE	198
Saviour, lead me, lest I stray	204	THE SHEPHERD TRUE	49
SAVIOUR, MORE THAN LIFE	220	THE SHIP OF TEMPERANCE	155
SAY "YES" TO JESUS NOW	22	THE TRUSTING HEART	78
See the place where Jesus lay	24	The weary hours like shadows	51
SEND THE LIGHT	229	There comes to my heart one	121
SHALL YOU? SHALL I?	142	THERE IS A GREEN HILL	125
SHIRLAND. S. M.	186	There is a land beyond the stars	234
Sinners Jesus will receive	167	There is a place of refuge	232
SOLDIERS OF THE KING	30	THERE IS NEVER A DAY SO DREARY	122
Some day the silver cord will	118	There is no friend like Jesus	93
Some one will enter the pearly	142	THERE'LL BE NO DARK VALLEY	106
SOME SWEET MORN	12	THERE SHALL BE SHOWERS OF	196
SOMETIME WE'LL UNDERSTAND	169	There's a call comes ringing o'er	229
Soul of mine in earthly temple	190	There's a royal banner given for	230
Sowing in the morning, sowing	209	THERE'S A WIDENESS	252
SPEED AWAY	136	There's sunshine in my soul	44
SPIRIT SO HOLY	23	There were ninety and nine that	198
STILL, STILL WITH THEE	259	They tell me of a land so fair	69

	No.		No
Thou Art My Life	103	When God the way of life	201
Thou Art My Rock	71	When I shall wake in that fair	224
Thou art, O, Lord, my hiding	37	When Jesus Comes Again	38
Thou, whose hand thus far	70	When my life-work is ended	126
Tho' Your Sins be as Scarlet	182	When the King Shall Come	75
Through the shining gate	114	When the Mists Have Rolled	138
Throw Out the Life-Line	147	When the Roll is Called	249
Thy God Reigneth	107	When the Saints are Marching	114
'Tis Midnight	208	When the sinner turns	6
Toplady. 7s, 6 lines	216	When the thick clouds intervene	20
To the Rescue	242	When the trumpet of the Lord	249
To Thee, who from the narrow	210	When we walk with the Lord	156
Trembling soul, beset by fears	107	Where is My Boy To-Night?	255
True-Hearted! Whole-Hearted!	131	Where is my wandering boy	255
Trust and Obey	156	Where My Redeemer Leads	13
		Where my Saviour's hand is	256
Under His Wings	5	Where My Saviour Leads	256
Upon the western plain	112	Where the Saviour Leads	58
		Who Are These?	227
Walking in the Sunshine	41	Whoever receiveth the Crucified	162
We are building in sorrow or joy	176	Who Is on the Lord's Side?	248
We Come, O Lord, to Thee	31	Whosoever Shall Call	91
We praise Thee, O God	241	Why Waitest Thou?	251
We're soldiers of the King	30	Willing to own Thee Master and	29
We Shall Meet	239	Without Thee, my Saviour	50
Welcome, Wanderer, Welcome	197	With the glorious morning	27
What a blessed hope is mine	98	Wonderful Love!	246
What a fellowship, what a joy	254	Woodworth. L. M.	213
What a Friend Thou Art	55	Would you be forever blest?	76
What a Friend We Have	140		
What a Wonderful Saviour	134	Ye Christian Heralds, Go	72
What means this eager, anxious	149a	"Ye shall know;" O word of	57

www.ingramcontent.com/pod-product-compliance
Lightning Source LLC
Chambersburg PA
CBHW031746230426
43669CB00007B/511